NEW FASHION
AND DESIGN
TECHNOLOGIES

First published 2009 by
Parramon Ediciones S.A.
Rosselló i Porcel, 21, 9th floor
08016 Barcelona

This English-language edition published 2010 by
A&C Black Publishers
36 Soho Square
London W1D 3QY
www.acblack.com

ISBN 978 1 408 12381 2

Cover design by James Watson

NEW FASHION AND DESIGN TECHNOLOGIES

Jose Antonio Guerrero

A&C BLACK • LONDON

A book on the application of new technologies to fashion design is needed more than ever but is also increasingly difficult to write. It is needed because the creative industry has proven itself more than equal to the task of advancing in all design, production and communication processes by using tools to galvanise and expand its potential. However, the speed and variety of innovation of new tools and applications in this booming market make it a challenge to stay abreast of the latest developments.

For those of us who were born without scanners or printers, drawing or photographic software, the changes in the last few decades have truly revolutionised our methods of work, and we are anticipating further developments to be made at any time. The use of personal computers has become widespread and they now constitute a fundamental tool for our generation regardless of the kind of work we do. However, the use of personal computers is particularly crucial in the area of design, where the development of global digital communication is fundamental.

Since the 1990s cutting-edge technology, particularly digital and data processing technology related to the Internet, has been embraced by advertising, fashion and industrial designers. Nowadays this technology is an indispensable tool in making the process of design creation, development and management more agile.

The rapid diffusion of new technologies and their incorporation into the business world has been triggered by several factors. One is the trend of subcontracting or outsourcing, whereby a company assigns particular functions or tasks – either internal or external – to a service company. This requires an improvement in communication systems and channels to facilitate communication between the various creative teams. Another factor is the consolidation of different software applications, such as image processing, drawing, video and communication, which offer today's designers a wide range of work possibilities unimaginable just a few decades ago. Lastly, communication between users and their computers has been improved; a greater number of available tools make the system more accessible, understandable and manageable. Thus many young designers no longer perceive the technical component of the programs as an insurmountable obstacle.

In the course of this book we will explain what these tools are and how to use the new systems to improve and facilitate results. The best way to understand these applications is to follow the work process through all the stages of creation, from the initial idea to the final marketing. The book features highly motivating projects which illustrate all the creative stages of a product. For each stage we analyse how the various labels or designers tackle the challenge of implementing their fashion design ideas. To offer a broader perspective of the integrated process of creation, production and communication of a fashion product, we have worked alongside fashion industry professionals from around the world who through their work have helped us to illustrate each of the key stages within the whole project. They have all kindly contributed their work and have shared their experiences with us.

Rather than appraising the projects featured, we analyse their experience within the fashion industry today, starting with the creative process and ending with communication.

In order to provide the reader with further information, the book also includes brief notes of a more technical nature which supplement the general text, and an analysis of individuals and companies' methods of work in the fashion industry. This books aims to combine both educational and technical material and to illustrate how this is applied through the examples and experience of prominent designers.

We would like to thank all those who have contributed by sharing with us their work, which forms the core of this book. Our aim is to provide the readers of this book with the necessary solutions, tools and methods they need to broaden their interest in fashion design, and develop and optimise their work in the field.

DESIGN

The beginning of the collection

For designers the most exciting stage of a project is precisely the beginning, the phase of conceptualisation. Here the initial ideas and images are generated which serve as inspiration and as a starting point for the design proposal from which the rest of the work evolves. The original idea might be inspired by a novel, a historical period, a piece of music, a style of painting or nature itself. Each designer looks for their muses, anywhere and everywhere.

Compilation of images

Images are a source of inspiration for fashion designers, because of their aesthetics, the shapes they evoke and their colours, which suggest potential chromatic combinations and harmonies. Any picture containing aesthetically suggestive elements is useful.

A designer begins to shape a project by collecting images and interleaving them in a way so as to give expression to his or her creative idea.

In the early stages, the design team or individual creators need to structure the development of their work. Inspiration boards or moodboards are created for this purpose. This stage of conceptualisation denotes the start of the creation of a design or collection.

It's important to emphasise the great impact that the new techniques of scanning, photo retouching and assembly of collages have had on this process; nowadays almost all designers use this technology. It portrays their initial ideas in a clear and definitive way that can be understood by the development and product team and provide a real starting point for them to work towards the final realisation of these initial ideas.

Traditionally, these compilations were made with various cuttings (photographs, pictures from magazines, fabric swatches and trims, initial sketches, etc.) that were fastened to a stand (with pins or glue) to give an overview of the collection. With the emergence of new computer applications and especially changes in working habits and tools (more powerful equipment, diverse geographical locations and tighter development timings) use of digital boards has increased. In this way work can be shared between all the team members electronically wherever they are, both rapidly and optimally.

There is no one single approach used in the industry for creating these boards; however we can highlight some main areas that need to be taken into account. The creation of concept and inspiration boards must always be based on the premise that we are working with upcoming seasons and therefore that they need to offer new ideas and new challenges which can surprise and stimulate inspiration and creativity. Trend boards are an important tool commonly used to supplement information, showing the colour and chromatic atmosphere of the collection (colour harmonies, combinations and contrasts, etc.). Neither should a good moodboard for the collection be omitted. This will represent all the cultural indicators relating to each concept (for each specific collection), from artistic or architectural work to books, comics, film images or concepts linked to emerging trends that may influence our future collection. Once the conceptual environment of the collection is defined, the first rough drafts for the creations must be started, usually referred to as the sketchbook. In many cases designers resort to the creation of collages, interpretations and variations of shapes that they have developed on their moodboards. The use of scanned images confers us with great freedom to recreate complex shapes, significantly simplifying the enormous task of compiling and simulating creative ideas in quick sketches, and with a powerful form of representation.

Moodboard for the Connect trend,
Spring / Summer 09.
© WGSN www.wgsn.com

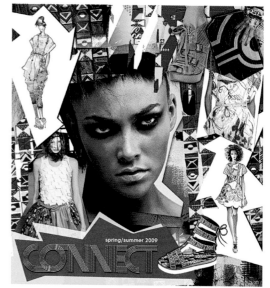

The elements included in the collage for the 'Connect'
trend Spring / Summer 09 are shown below. These have
been blended using Photoshop layers and layer masks to
form a complete picture.

CROP AND STRAIGHTEN PHOTOGRAPHS IN SCANNING

With the new and improved tools for importing of images in Adobe Photoshop, you can place several photographs in the scanner and scan them in one pass, which creates a single image file. The Crop and Straighten Photos command is an automated feature that can create individual image files from the multiple-image scan.

For best results, you shouldn't put the photographs too close together – it's better to leave a gap of a few millimetres between the images in your scan, and the background (the scanner bed) should be a uniform colour with little noise, otherwise cover the bottom with coloured cardboard. You need to do this because the Crop and Straighten Photos command works best on images with clearly delineated outlines.

When we are closer to the final product, fabric boards can be made to display materials (fabric, tricot, trims, etc.) and garments details, as well as initial ideas of prominent shapes, volumes, style ideas and combinations of garments.

For collections with a large component of prints and patterns it is important to present boards showing the general character of the collection, in order to assess the balance and consistency of the proposals within the overall concept. Some professional companies (such as WGSN) provide their clients with trend boards through their online services. Their work clearly indicates a trend and the way forward for the fashion industry.

SEARCHING FOR INFORMATION ON THE INTERNET

The top search engines like Google, Yahoo!, Altavista, Windows Live or Ask, and the infinite variations on them, are applications that browse the network, indexing information in their vast databases. The speed and degree of success of a search depends on specific software known as a Web robot or Web crawler. These are programs whose function is to compile information on the content, structure and keywords of the websites they come across. The principal search engines have their own Web robots (such as Googlebot and Msnbot) that browse for information according to different criteria. While they may attract visitors to a site, they also have the disadvantage that their insistent data search can lead to the website collapsing.

At present, the leadership of major search engines such as Google or Yahoo seems indisputable. Whilst new platforms are emerging that could become competitive in the medium term or not too distant future, like MySpace or Baidu, for the time being they have no contenders. Google and Yahoo both have an aggressive and very active acquisitions policy, which situates them in the forefront of all Internet-related developments. If there is any innovation on the Internet, these two browsers are behind it.

The author says about his work: 'I search for information on the Internet, in books, magazine articles, etc. When I've got enough material I start to put the images together, since most of them are in digital format (if not, I scan them) and I use Adobe Photoshop to juxtapose them. I paste them into a blank document and play around with them. Using the computer you've got total freedom, and as you work with the collages, the concepts and the atmosphere improve and evolve, generating different ideas that help to enhance the work. Apart from forming the start of the project, these compositions using Photoshop are also a presentation and a graphic communication of the project.'

Composition. *Spring in Mesopotamia* Project.
© Icaro Néstor Ibáñez Arricivita, 2008.

CARO NÉSTOR IBÁÑEZ ARRICIVITA

After seeing Lauren Bacall sketching dresses in Vincente Minnelli's film *Designing Woman* (1957), he decided to devote his life to drawing original and creative dresses. From there, he graduated in Textile Design and Fashion from the ESDI School (Barcelona). Today he is completing his studies at the Royal Academy of Fine Arts in Antwerp (Belgium).

He has worked with designers such as Lutz Huelle and Bernhard Willhelm, whom he thanks, among others, for a significant part of his personal and artistic growth. Currently Icaro Néstor continues drawing and collaborating on artistic projects from his habitual place of work in Antwerp.

www.myspace.com/icaroh

VERTICAL SEARCH ENGINES

Vertical or topical search engines have emerged with the aim of making better use of the information that the Web robots provide. They are specialised in specific areas, which means that they produce a smaller number of results but which are more accurate, useful and profitable. The vertical search engine robots only browse websites with content related to a specific topic, which favours more efficient searches and more frequent browsing of content, and therefore they can offer more up-to-date information.

The interface of vertical search engines can incorporate resources and tools tailored to the user's specific needs, which can sometimes be very useful, as, for instance, in the case of image or video browsers, such as the popular Youtube. Examples of this type of applications are blog search engines such as the acclaimed Technorati, which allows us to restrict our search to the growing world of the 'blogosphere', its rival Google Blog Search, Icerocket or the Spanish Agregax, or the video search engines or image search engines referred to previously such as Picsearch, Pikeo or the essential Flickr, to name only a few of the most well-known.

In vertical search engines the links are ranked in order of relevance, as determined by the specific algorithms of each search engine. These take into account characteristics such as the volume of traffic or the quantity and quality of the links to the site and up to 200 other variables. We can say that algorithms form the heart of the browser, on which the success of each search depends. For this reason companies keep the algorithms of each search engine a closely guarded secret and invest in their research and development, so that they are subject to continuous changes to improve the quality of their relevance criteria and to improve their security to avoid them being decrypted and copied. The browser's prestige depends on the reliability and independence of its algorithms.

The Internet has a growing number of vertical search engines and this means that in turn, 'search engines for search engines' are beginning to proliferate, such as the Spanish Buscopio, which aim to establish order among so much variety. Google itself seems to have realised the need for more specialised searches, and has launched the applications Google Custom Search Engine and Google Co-op, which allow the integration and construction of customised search engines based on the Google search engine. In the case of Google Co-op, as well as being able to select your chosen website addresses to search for information, it includes collaborative tools, which allow search refinements to be made through users' 'collective intelligence' such as Web 2.0.

1 Details of the design studio of the young designer Domingo Ayala. Photographs © Mari Luz Vidal.

2 Photography exhibition of the photography project developed by www.hel-looks.com in the gallery Bingoshop, Barcelona. Photographs © Mari Luz Vidal.

TECHNORATI is much more than a browser, it's practically a portal dedicated to blogs and their content. Technorati has become the most popular search engine aimed at the blogosphere. The main difference between a general search engine such as Google and Technorati relates to time: Google sorts results by relevance while Technorati also values if sites have been recently updated. You can run a basic search in Technorati by entering keywords in the search box on the home page. However, the tags feature is more convenient for searches. Tags can be used in two ways, either by visiting the official Technorati Tags site or using the drop-down menu. The Tags page is very useful in allowing you to view the hottest issues in the blogosphere in real time – the words are displayed in a larger font. As we have already mentioned, the results of a Technorati search change every minute, and the most recently updated blogs appear first. At this stage, search engines have become too valuable as tools to leave in the hands of Web robots and algorithms. It is clear that to date no search engine can compete with a 'human' expert's ability for semantic selection and analysis. Everything points to future search engines combining automated searches and those based on human criteria. In the case of vertical search engines dealing with highly specialised topics, only human selection can make sense of the information. Therefore automated search technologies are often complemented by the criteria of users, who classify the information using tags. The information is stored in the order chosen by the user, allowing a more organised and controlled search.

Detail of the design studio of the designer Pink Olive. Here attractive sketches and fashion collections are produced based on illustrations. Photograph © Mari Luz Vidal.

HOW DO SEARCH ENGINE ROBOTS WORK?
When you run a search in a browser, it checks the databases created with the information compiled by the robots and, based on this, automatically generates a list of results. The result of this process is an enormous amount of information. The problem is that any search generates hundreds of thousands of useless results, given that statistics show that the user only consults the first 10 or 20 links at most.

TAGS
A tag refers to a keywords or label. The keyword can be compared to an image or computer file that can be found through browsing or searching on the Internet. The distinctive feature of tags is that they are personal and can be freely chosen by the author or user. The action of tagging files is closely related to Web 2.0 sites, which were pioneers in the use of tags. Tagging enables website databases to grow in a decentralised way.

Images that are references for many designers of casual wear developing their prints.

The Record Room album with 1,854 record covers, created by Bradley Loos.

IMAGE AND VIDEO HOSTING WEBSITES

There are currently various applications available for organising and sharing images at no cost using powerful tools. The main feature of these services is to share pictures across the world. The user can choose under what conditions to share ('Copyright', open licences or the various types of 'Copyleft' provided by Creative Commons). These systems provide improved systems for classification of images using tags, which are simply words that associate an image with a definition, topic or concept.

This makes it easier for us to find our own photographs and those of other users, and to select images based on our interests. Many of these services also allow you to upload and view the photographs as a presentation.

Among the best-known managers, the most prominent are Flickr (with more than two billion images), Favshare, Pikeo, Zooomr, Photobucket or Myalbum.

CREATIVE COMMONS defines itself as a non-profit organisation which is dedicated to reducing the legal obstacles to creativity. The aim of their work is to achieve a legal model which uses computing tools to facilitate the use and distribution of work out of copyright. The Creative Commons or CC Licences are based on the General Public Licence (GPL) of the Free Software Foundation. The licences have had to be adapted to various legal systems around the world, as they were originally only in English.

The various Creative Commons licences base their principles of authorship on:

- **ATTRIBUTION:** requires users to cite the source of the work. The author must appear in the credits.

- **NON-COMMERCIAL:** requires that the work available to users is not used for commercial purposes and there is no financial gain for anyone who makes use of this licence.

- **NO DERIVATIVES:** prevents the work from being distributed with modifications, i.e. the content must not be changed.

- **SHARE-ALIKE:** All derived works must always be distributed under the same licence as the original work.

FLICKR WWW.FLICKR.COM

Flickr is perhaps one of the most useful tools for searching for images. It is an application for organising and sharing photographs, drawings and other kinds of creations online. Flickr has a remarkable image-sharing community that has millions of users and hundreds of millions of available photographs and videos. The application has two principal objectives. The first is to help the user make material available to other individuals who are interested, and it allows photographs and videos to be uploaded both inside and outside the system, i.e. from the Web, from mobile devices, from personal computers, or any other software with the capacity to manage them. Secondly, the content can be accessed in several ways, including through the Flickr website, by e-mail, posting on external blogs, etc. Given this, we can say that Flickr's system offers the best tools for managing and sharing photographs and video files in a very interactive format.

This popular website is used as a personal server for sharing personal photographs and the service is used worldwide by bloggers as a photo repository.

Part of Flickr's popularity is due to the large online community accessing the service, as well as the tools that allow authors to tag their photographs, and an explore section with the best photographs of the week. Currently Flickr hosts more than two billion images. The service is widely used by bloggers as a repository of photographs and videos. The Flickr system allows you to make image and video searches on the basis of tags, dates, and Creative Commons licences.

Flickr accounts are intended for personal use of members for sharing their own photographs and videos. There are also Flickr groups, where a number of users form a group based on a common interest. The groups are either public, where you can join by invitation, or completely private. Each group has a pool for sharing photographs and videos and an image for discussion. If you can't find a Flickr group for the topic that interests you, you have the option of creating a new group.

Flickr is also used like a social network, i.e. it offers the option of directly contacting the user, as well as adding personal details to individual profiles. Flickr can serve as a fundamental search engine to contact potential professional contacts (other designers, graphic artists, suppliers, etc.).

A UNIVERSAL APPLICATION

It was developed by Ludicorp, a Canadian company, founded in 2002 in Vancouver. It was launched in February 2004, initially as a game where several players could take part online. The first versions of Flickr included the feature FlickrLive, which was a chat room which allowed photographs to be exchanged in real time. The success of this feature gradually led to a greater focus on the exchange of photographs and implementation of new features for individual users. Over time the exchange of photographs became firmly established and the chat room was finally eliminated. In March 2005, Flickr and Ludicorp were acquired by the giant Yahoo!

The superiority of Flickr's features led Yahoo! to abandon its Yahoo! Photographs system, which had become somewhat dated, to develop the resources of the very popular Flickr site. On July 11, 2007, Flickr was translated into seven more languages, making it even more popular and more accessible.

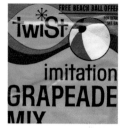

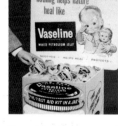

Fashion media groups on the Web

The online publications of the major fashion media groups have also had a tremendous impact on the task of searching for images. Media and fashion firms now have their own interactive portals for communication with their target audience.

This type of portals offers you the option of viewing videos which may range from fashion shows and photo shoots to backstage scenes at fashion shows of the most important industry labels. Television projects are also appearing on the Internet, and have become an area specialised in images and videos and a space for social participation.

In September 2000, CondéNet, the online services division of the Condé Nast group (owner of publications as well-established as *Vogue, Vanity Fair, The New Yorker, Allure* or *Glamour*) launched the websites style.com and men.style.com. These include more than 50,000 photographs covering fashion shows, videos, trends, forums, newsletters, as well as social and cultural information. The information is updated daily and includes spaces for sharing views and participation. Other groups, such as *Elle, Nylon, R & D magazine, Wallpaper*, etc. have also developed similar digital projects: www.elle.es, www.nylonmag.com, www.i-dmagazine.com, www.wallpaper.com.

In fact, we can confirm that all the current market leaders specialising in style and fashion now have their own portal. The trend, however, is to what are referred to as interactive websites. Whereas initially publications' websites were used for displaying material, currently the major publishing groups are developing websites in which the reader actively participates in the content. One of the points of references in this is the website created by the French group Hachette Filipacchi which has been a genuine revolution in France: www.veryelle.elle.fr.

It is a modern version of the website of its flagship publication (*Elle*) whose pages all offer the visitor opportunities to take part: from discovering the thousand and one combinations featured in the selection of trends made by the magazine's fashion team, to enjoying the very latest music or listening to live interviews with well-known personalities in society and culture. The most significant features of these specialised fashion websites are their pace and their universal appeal (as well as easy access to the information).

In short, it's about bringing fashion into the real world: combing the streets of the major capitals of the fashion world (London, New York, Paris, Milan or Tokyo) in search of people who embody the current design trend. On occasions it's not a question of photographing and observing interesting people on the street, rather those same people introducing themselves and choosing to experience the scrutiny of visitors to the website, who will also find, besides the description of the garments, an account of the target style of the individual featured. Moreover, in less than 24 hours from the presentation of any product, event or show, information is available regarding the launch of international collections, as well as any issues relating to the major fashion labels (launches, advertising, campaigns, collaborations, etc.) which are responsible for setting market trends.

1 Image of catwalk
Dolce & Gabanna, Autumn / Winter 08. © WGSN.

2 Image of catwalk
Emma Cook Autumn / Winter 08. © WGSN.

3 Image of catwalk
Nathan Jenden, Autumn / Winter 08. © WGSN.

The media impact of many well-known prestigious
models is not confined to the catwalks and fashion
shows. They are literally hounded in their everyday
activities and therefore become indicators of the
trends and combinations that will be more easily
assimilated on the street.

INTERACTIVE SPACES

The information found on the online
communication services of the fashion media
groups tends to vary from what appears in
traditional printed media. The websites aim to
offer more direct, familiar and user-interactive
information. They also incorporate various
small applications to encourage audience
loyalty (video downloads, music, forums,
areas for views and participation, etc.).

Trends, markets and street culture

The emergence and expansion of new media has been, without a doubt, one of the most important factors in the democratisation of fashion. They have made thousands of images of designs and collections accessible to everybody. In fact, 'you can't feel the pulse of the world of fashion without devouring blogs and websites,' according to the stylist Cristina M. Faber.

The unlimited access to images on the Web has a strange feedback effect. It's hard to know if the photographs on the Web reflect the style previously dictated by the designers, or if it is the collections that are inspired by the latest far-fetched innovations circulating in cyberspace.

This question is probably difficult to answer; however, it's unarguable that certain blogs and websites have a tremendous impact on the world of style, fabrics, prints and accessories. This, together with their increasing influence, means that we need to redefine their role and especially their relationship with the traditional media.

THE IMPACT OF BLOGS

Blogs form a central part of Internet culture. The world of fashion absorbs approximately 10% of all the websites in the global system (according to Technorati, the specialised blog search engine mentioned in the preceding chapter). In them, Madonna's impeccable wardrobe coexists with the latest collection of Marc Jacobs accessories, a mixture where quality is not always consistent. However, there are some blogs which stand out from the multitude of choices as prominent and respected in fashion today: *Vogue, Elle* or *Nylon* magazines have been pioneers in the use of blogs to customise content and adapt it to the increasingly specific profile of their readers.

Streets and young people are the best reflection of where trends are going.
© icanteachyouhowtodoit.
www.icanteachyouhowtodoit.com

Page 25
Fashion websites show us what people are wearing in the big cities. Here, Helsinki.
© Hel-looks.
www.hel-looks.com

NEW COMMUNICATION CHANNELS
Recent studies show that the younger generation feels a strong detachment from television and traditional communication channels. They are more interested in the Internet, which has become the main tool of information and entertainment.

Internet becomes the new arena where contacts, famous people and advice coexist with catwalks, celebrities and trends. They exercise an indisputable influence over young people, and their existence has now shifted to cyberspace. Their behaviour, tastes and aesthetic influences are copied to the limit.

the city and especially of trends. So more than switching over from what was a simple hobby, I started to take everything more seriously, customising my assignments, building my confidence day-by-day, and always carrying my camera in my bag.'

All images © Verena Grotto.
appealtotheeye.blogspot.com

VERENA GROTTO began her work with an assignment from *H magazine* for their December 2007 issue. The subject was: 'What plans do you have for New Year's Eve?' 'They were the first photographs I had published in the mass media. After just a few months things started to take off. I had my first interview published on the website www.setyourstyle , which I'm working with now on some interviews and articles on the latest fashion, trends, music, etc.' She has also carried out numerous assignments for the Bulgarian magazine *Indie*, has contributed to the magazine *Vice Spain*, for an internal coolhunting job, to the Korean magazine *Cracker your wardrobe*, and to the Italian magazine *A*. Verena says: 'I normally get contacted through my blog, which has become my best advertisement.'

👤 APPEALTOTHEEYE.BLOGSPOT.COM
This is the project of a 21-year-old Italian, Verena Grotto, that includes, in addition to street photography, articles or information about bands and concerts.

In the designer's own words: 'Appeal to the eye began without any expectations. In June 2006 Stefano Rosso from DIESEL Italy took me to lunch. Being a great friend of mine, he asked if I could do coolhunting, i.e. act as a trendspotter based in Barcelona and send him a document each month with photographs taken on the streets of the city. He trusted my taste in fashion and my knowledge of

'Whenever I travel I like to come away with the essence of the modern spirit of the city I go to. I've been to Milan, Bassano del Grappa, London, Munich and Berlin, just for now; I've got plans to visit many others. The short timeframe I have doesn't let me do everything I'd like. But one thing that's certain is that whenever I get a photo opportunity, my finger is at the ready on the shutter.'

Agyness Deyn, backstage image. © WGSN.

Models are style icons that many people want to imitate. The Internet has a great deal of information that helps us to get to know them better. For example, Agyness Deyn, known by the British press as 'the Kate Moss successor', is featured in various blogs and websites that give details of her work, her style and her life.
www.nymag.com

The blog phenomenon is still on the rise; we are witnessing the dawn of the fifth estate. If the 20th century was the century of the press – the fourth estate – which counterbalanced the traditional public authorities, it is now blogs which are beginning to take up the role of protector of media independence. This idea is based on the loss of strength of the press as the fourth estate as a consequence of the emergence of the big media groups, and on the growing ability of blogs, with their independent nature, to fill the resulting gap. Blogs add greater versatility and intuition to the traditional media's solid make up. In fact, many digital media have their own blogs or foster them in various ways. An increasing number of journalists use blogs as a means of personal expression. Prime examples include sites such as the *The Sartorialist* (US), which brings together the photographs published by Scott Schuman in the platform of the magazine *GQ*. In his own words: 'I started taking pictures out of curiosity and created a website for sharing them in September 2005. I feel very proud to have fostered a constructive dialogue between fashion lovers.' His website has numerous images exhaustively documenting 'streetwear' trends, the urban fashion of New Yorkers, Milanese or Parisians. Like *The Sartorialist*, there are other websites such as the Japanese *Tokyo Street Style* or the English *London Street Fashion*, which also feature a daily journal of urban snapshots. These types of website are becoming a principal source of images for studying and analysing the current urban trends of different cities around the world. The work of the Finnish group Hel, who recently exhibited their work in Barcelona, is also worth noting. Their projects *Icanteachyouhowtodoit* and *Appealtotheeye* reflect the youngest and most vibrant scene in the major European cities.

New web tools for fashion

Some Internet sites have been able to benefit from the new circumstances of the textile industry (outsourcing, relocation, reduction of design and production times, etc.). We can see how the traditional international trade shows have given way to digital portals where, upon payment of a registration fee, the most up-to-the-minute industry information is permanently available.

There is an ever-increasing demand for services tailored to the new context which provide useful information regarding aspects such as trends, fashion shows, markets, graphics and printing, designers, trade shows or suppliers. The ability to access this information at any time and from our workplace is a valuable tool that shouldn't be underestimated.

Beyond the style or coolhunter sites, there are blogs – some more professional than others — with general fashion industry news, such as *Trendencias* (the number one Spanish language website, according to Google Rank's analysis). There are also some specialising in a single product such as *The bagsnob* (for bags and leather goods) or *Shoeblog* (women's footwear), or projects such as *The coolhunter* with comprehensive information on of all kinds of global trends, including references to interiors and visual merchandising. Future Concept Lab and WGSN are probably two of the most successful projects on the scene in recent years, and deserve a special mention.

FUTURE CONCEPT LAB

Future Concept Lab is an institute for research and conceptualisation that analyses global trends related to the most ground-breaking developments in the areas of design, marketing or communication. Its field of action extends from Europe and the United States to the emerging countries of Asia and South America (its analysis centres are spread over 25 countries). Its programme is the result of the tracking and analysis of the main media and the influence of trend-setters in each region with the aim of unearthing future social and cultural trends, etc. Fields such as music, literature or art are key parts of its research focused on future markets. One of FCL's main activities is the 'street and body signals' research area (SBS) for which 50 correspondents, experts in various fields, record the habits, attitudes and representations of fashion and style of specific population groups, in an attempt to unearth the most colourful and original behaviour. The SBS programme analysis is aimed at identifying the most innovative trends associated with the new 4P's of their research: people, places, plans and projects. The SBS project started in 1992 in the five major fashion capitals: Milan, Paris, London, New York and Tokyo, but has grown presently to more than 40 cities around the world, meaning that the company is able to offer comparative global information in real-time.

One of the services offered by Future Concept Lab
is run by a group of coolhunters that record their
observations of people's behaviour in order to identify the
latest trends. © Future Concept Lab
www.futureconceptlab.com

CREATIVE FACTORY
FCL's research allows their users to keep a
step ahead of future trends and strategies.
The institute, with headquarters in Milan,
offers consultancy, training and specific
research services. Furthermore, their activities
range from their own website to articles
published in various media. They have
recently published a book, *Real Fashion
Trends*, in which they examine and expand on
their work in recent years.

Images from the *Retail* directory.
© WGSN.

WGSN

International fashion shows are featuring digital portals that keep fashion professionals up to date with the latest innovations, instantaneously and from our workplace, following the payment of a charge for the service. Among these sites the undisputable leader is www.wgsn.com, a young and ambitious venture which has managed to respond to the industry's requirements like few others have. WGSN is the world's largest B2B Internet portal that operates as the foremost research and trend analysis service for the fashion, design and retail industries.

WGSN provides professionals with copious information on the current state of the fashion market. It has an international scope and its services have become global. It would otherwise have been impossible to absorb the costs of such an ambitious project and optimise the various services they offer: information on the latest trends, images of fashion shows with a wealth of detail, international market analysis, information on exhibitions, specialist designers or international suppliers, as well as any significant information related to the fashion industry.

Currently, WGSN operates as a tool that carries out an exhaustive study of consumer attitudes as well as a product's life cycle, from its conception and design to production and marketing. More than 200 fashion professionals, trend analysts, journalists and coolhunters with broad experience in leading market labels participate in this online project. The portal covers womenswear, menswear, childrenswear, accessories, footwear, interiors, youth fashion, denim, casual and sports fashion and sports and many others. They employ a great variety of references and sources that include advertising, architecture, media, lifestyles, workstyles, street fashion, health, entertainment, travel, sports, art, science, technology, gastronomy and cars, to name a few.

GLOBAL TRENDS

The company WGSN was founded in 1998 by Julian and Marc Worth, and was later acquired in 2005 by the company Emap plc. Its headquarters are in London but they also have centres of operations in the main international cities: New York, Hong Kong, Los Angeles, Paris, São Paulo, Istanbul, Barcelona, Melbourne, Tokyo, Milan, etc. It is precisely this global perspective that allows them to compile and reflect the trends as the signs emerge around the world, connecting different stories and indications in order to obtain an overview, look ahead to the future and think about what is behind the trends that they are predicting.

Isabel Mesa, Country Manager for Spain and Portugal talks about the some aspects of the WGSN project's future: 'Firstly it's worth noting the educational work being carried out with various colleges of fashion through the website wgsn-edu.com, which fosters the participation of young people. Furthermore, the portal is going to adopt a new application, an image browser for navigating around the more than 20,000 images they have, which are organised into themes such as colour, trend, materials, etc.' The website will soon feature video images of shows, parties and social events.

1

2

Images Retail Directory.
© WGSN.

WGSN Finder provides access to images of celebrity trend-setters. Here we can see the model Kate Moss (**1**) and the singer Victoria Beckham (**2**), two of the celebrities most sought after by the public who want to know what their idols are wearing, or by the media to show pictures of these two style icons.

The portal is structured in a very simple menu based on directories (it currently has 16 sub-sections) which include information specific to each subject. Some of the directories are highlighted here as examples.

Think Tank with seasonal research two years in advance: colour, graphics, materials, textiles, macrotrends, consumer attitudes, and so on.

Trends includes seasonal research, trends and product directions (colour, shape, materials, graphics, inspiration and packages of product development) for womenswear, menswear, childrenswear, accessories, footwear, lingerie/swim and denim.

Graphics with a gallery of collections of transfer prints and direct positioning, reports, inspiration, clipart.

Materials dedicated to information and reports of fabric samples for seasons, trade shows, etc.

Catwalks a huge display of large-format images of the catwalks of New York, London, Paris and Milan with four types of analysis (by themes, colours, fabrics, garments, cities, etc.).

What's in store an analysis and photographs of products on sale at point of sale (more than 10,000 photographs per month).

Youth / Junior studies of trends in the juvenile market, reports, inspiration and a street fashion series (one report per week).

City by City has practical information and travel guides for designers, art exhibitions, restaurants, clubs, hotels, etc.

Generation Now what the youngest and freshest designers have to offer, with shows and information on graduates from the best schools of design (CSM, Parsons, etc.).

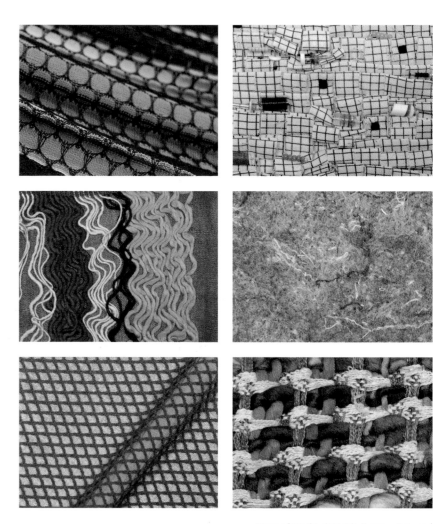

Images from the *Materials* directory, Autumn / Winter 2010, which feature various fabric samples representing the season's trends.
© WGSN

Images from the *Materials* directory, Autumn / Winter 2010, which feature various fabric samples representing the season's trends. © WGSN.

The Street Trends directory contains images of young people as an illustration of different dress styles. © WGSN.

TRENDS DIRECTORY

The Trends directory of WGSN is perhaps the most popular section of the website's menu. The predictions shown on www.wgsn.com reflect the most significant product directions for future seasons in relation to issues such as colour, fabric, shapes and volumes of the garments. Trends' predictions can subsequently be found appearing on catwalks, shows and in retail.

The different sections of this directory are:

WOMENSWEAR AND MENSWEAR directions on influences, colour, fabric and design.

INTIMATE APPAREL / SWIMWEAR specific information for the lingerie textile industry on issues such as colours, textures, trims, details.

KIDSWEAR the latest for children; includes applied printing and graphics.

FOOTWEAR footwear for men and women, the latest in shapes, materials and technical innovations.

ACCESSORIES with special attention to handbags, belts, leather goods, plus jewellery, eyewear and watches.

DENIM with the latest in washing systems for denim, trims, applications and design directions.

COLOUR palettes and ranges for future seasons.

INTERIORS homewear trends.

PRODUCTION

Project development

After the process of conceptualisation and search for information is concluded, we begin the phase of bringing the work to life. To do so, we need to transform the idea into a design from which the actual prototype can be created. This can be done in many different ways, and there is more than one recipe for success. There is a wide range of available tools from which we have to learn how to make the right choices to achieve the desired result. In the course of this section we will examine the work of various designers and design firms, from examples of the depiction of whole figures in certain media, to 2D drawings with all the garment description parameters.

ALL YOU NEED
TO BE A DESIGNER

I ♥ YOU

ALL YOU NEED
TO BE A DESIGNER

High-tech or traditional techniques

It is unlikely that computer programs will ever be able to replace the spontaneity and immediacy of traditional art techniques such as the pencil or paintbrush. However, it is essential to note the increasingly important role that digital processes are playing in completing the representation of designs.

Computer software is intended to be just this: yet another drawing instrument, featuring multiple tools for colour adjustment, retouching, editing, etc., to create a wide range of effects and different types of processing, which properly used, can offer a clearer and more realistic representation of the object. It is common to merge different techniques in the design process, for instance to draw or colour the first rough sketches by hand, then to scan these images and complete them with digital techniques. There are also examples of designers who carry out the whole design process on the computer, both in 2D (line drawing, false perspective or flat drawing) or in 3D, which enables a design to be presented from all possible angles. Nowadays with the existing software you can colour a scanned sketch or photograph, modify an image for creative purposes or add both flat (2D) and three-dimensional (3D) elements created entirely by computer applications.

The use of computer applications in the design process does not, as might be assumed, produce a more mechanical and colder representation – very personal and artistic images can be created using this procedure. In the same way that a photographer is fully aware of the features and potential of his or her camera, a designer using digital technology exploits the potential of the applications and the media to achieve creative representations full of character, which are every bit as good as results obtained using traditional painting techniques. Just as no two photographs are the same, nor are any two designs – even if they have been developed using the same instruments, the hand and mind of the designer are still, in both cases, decisive.

POTENTIAL OF COMPUTER-BASED DESIGN TECHNIQUES

The numerous techniques offered by design software give designers greater freedom and open up new possibilities in the creation of a design. The main advantages this tool offers are:

- The ability to modify or alter the image without this changing its presentation.

- To compose designs using different kinds of elements and then apply a uniform shape and colour to the composition that would take a lot more work with traditional paint.

- To work in layers and handle each element separately, offering a much greater and more thorough control over the image content.

- The system is also convenient for storing work and facilitates communication between the various creative teams via email.

Apple T-shirt designed by Kustaa Saksi (Paris) using
digital technology for The Photo Gallery.
© thgallery /www.thgallery.fr

TYPES OF IMAGE

The programs developed for the design industry interpret an 'image' as an encrypted file containing a visual representation of something (a photograph, a graphic element, a sketch, etc.). Depending on the code defining the image, different results are created with their own characteristics.

RASTERISED IMAGES OR BITMAPS

Rasterised images are made up of small coloured squares called pixels, which are combined like tiles in a mosaic to create a picture. These images are sometimes called raster images, or also bitmaps or pixmaps. Photographs, scanned images or graphics created with paint programs are all examples of bitmaps, and are viewable by a monitor, on paper or any other display medium.

Bitmaps are usually technically identified by the height and width of the image (in pixels) and by the colour depth (in bits per pixel), which determines the number of different colours that can be stored in each pixel and thus, to a great extent, points to the colour quality of the image.

The bitmap format is very widespread and is generally used for taking digital photographs and video shots. Analogue-to-digital conversion devices, such as scanners and digital cameras, are used for this purpose. Each pixel has its own colour; the images in the RGB colour model (red, green, blue), for example, are composed of pixels of three bytes. One byte for each colour: red, green and blue. Simpler images require less information per pixel, for example, an image composed only of black and white pixels requires just one bit per pixel (1 if it is black and 0 if it is white).

PIXELS, THE SMALLEST UNIT

Pixel is the acronym of 'picture element' and is the smallest homogeneous colour unit that forms part of a digital image, whether it's a photograph, a video still frame or a graphic image. They are defined as geometric units, small squares or rectangles that are coloured, white or black, or shades of gray. If you zoom in sufficiently on a digital image you can distinguish them – you'll see the image is made up of a grid of pixels.

Therefore, images are made up of a rectangular grid, where each pixel takes up a relatively small segment of the total image. Enlarging the format and resolution of your documents may cause the quality of pixel-based images to deteriorate, so it is essential to take into account the dimensions the final file will have before starting to work with it.

M.Bee's various projects use techniques as simple as the juxtapositioning of different images, generating a background colour under a more line-based drawing, or the synthesis of several illustrations in a final piece.

1 *Qu'est-ce que c'est l'amour?* 2007 © m.Bee. Part of the *Portraitizm* project.

2 *Lady in furs*. 2007 © m.Bee. Part of the *Portraitizm* project. Mixed media.

3 *The mad park*. 2007 © m.Bee. Part of the *Mashimotta* project.

M.BEE

M.Bee is Maria Balashowa. The artist's work combines all the tools available to her. Two years ago she started work on *Portraitizm*, which illustrates current fashion, taking as her reference point trends among young people on the streets of her city, paying particular attention to the garments, accessories and the style of her characters.

www.myspace.com/mbee_mary
www.flickr.com/photos/balashowa

PRINT QUALITY
Nowadays standard computer screens show between 72 and 130 pixels per inch, and some printers print 2,400 dots per inch or more. It is rather difficult to decide what the best image resolution is for a printer. It is important to bear in mind that the printout may show greater detail than is visible on the computer screen.

The total number of pixels determines the resolution of a rasterised image, and the amount of information in each pixel (colour depth) determines the image quality. The resolution of an image indicates how much detail can be seen in it. For example, an image that stores 24 bits of colour information per pixel (the standard for screens since 1995) can portray more shades of colour than an image that only stores 16 bytes per pixel, but will not have same amount of detail as one that stores 48 bits per pixel. Thus, an image with a resolution of 640 x 480 pixels (therefore containing 307,200 pixels) seems rougher and of lower quality than an image of 1280 x 1024 (1,310,720 pixels). Since storing high quality images requires a great deal of space, image processing programs often use data compression techniques to reduce their size. Some of these techniques sacrifice information and consequently image quality in order to save disc space. The technical term for this technique is irreversible or 'lossy' data compression.

REQUIREMENTS FOR THE RESOLUTION
OF BITMAP IMAGES
Bitmap images contain a fixed number of pixels, which are usually measured in pixels per inch or dpi (dot per inch). A high-resolution image contains more pixels than a low-resolution image of same size, therefore the pixels are smaller. As a point of reference regarding the requirements for image resolution, commercial printing requires images of 150 to 300 dpi, which is the standard resolution. Most professional printers work with images of at least 150 dpi, especially since the Computer to Plate (CTP) preprinting technique has been massively implemented, which eliminates the photolithography process.

The fact that commercial printing requires high-resolution images is a problem for the designer since the large size of these images slows down the computer and they take longer to be displayed. It is best to work with low-resolution versions and then replace them with high-resolution images for printing. During the design process it's common to work with images of a lower resolution than those that will finally be used (72 dpi for photographs printed on a 300 dpi printer, 150 dpi for photographs printed on printers with up to 1,000 dpi), which makes work quicker and more flexible. When preparing the final document the low-resolution images are automatically replaced by their high-resolution counterparts. Online i.e. Internet publishing often requires images to have pixel dimensions that match the monitor. They are normally less than 500 pixels wide and 400 pixels high, allowing space for the browser window controls and other page design elements, such as captions for illustrations.

1 *Dance* © 2008 Teresa Hu.

2 *Slumber Party* © 2008 Teresa Hu (part of Pink Series).

3 *La Cucaracha* © 2008 Teresa Hu.
Her work combines traditional ink drawing with the digital possibilities of Photoshop, which features various tools for painting or editing the colour of an image. With the painting tools, she can change the colour of the pixels in the image, retouch images, create or edit masks in alpha channels or paint original illustrations. Brush tips, standard brushes and many of the brush options give creative control for producing impressive paint effects or simulating work with traditional media.

TERESA HU
Teresa Hu is the name used by Leoluca Escobar, an illustrator from Los Angeles. After studying at the Art Center College of Design she moved to Berlin where she currently works. Her illustrations reflect on the fashion and attitudes of young people.

www.leolucaescobar.com

Graphic interpretations of popular icons are a distinctive trait in popular youth culture nowadays. This is the case of heidi.com's direct prints, featuring the face of the popular Heidi.
It has been simplified with plain-coloured geometric shapes, in the style of Japanese dolls. The vector representation of drawings with thick outlines and rounded shapes,are key to their development.

Images from the Summer 08 collection, www.heidi.com

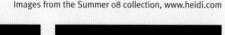

HEIDI.COM

The brand was created in 2003 by a Swiss firm, which decided to evoke the greatest times of the icon of Heidi in the Swiss Alps. They began their career distributing the designs on the Internet, but rapidly received product orders from a multitude of shops, so that the project has grown to its current situation. Today the products are distributed in more than 120 stores worldwide, and are present at most international trade shows.

The collection includes T-shirts, sweatshirts, jackets, etc.; generally casual and comfortable clothes. The central icons are the graphics based on the character of Heidi, interpreted by the artists with complete freedom and a sense of humour.

www.heidi.com

VECTOR IMAGE

A vector image is a digital image made up of independent geometric objects (segments, polygons, arcs, etc.), each defined by the different mathematical attributes of their shape, position, colour, etc. For example, a green circle would be characterised by the location of its centre point, its radius, its stroke line thickness and its colour.

The vector format is entirely different from the format of pixel-based images. The main advantage of vector graphics is that an image can be freely enlarged without suffering the scaling effect of
images formed by pixels. Vector graphics therefore allow images to be moved, stretched and twisted in a relatively simple way.

Vector drawing creates lines called paths. A path is made up of one or more straight or curved segments. The beginning and the end of each segment are marked by anchor points, which act like pins holding a wire in place. A path may be closed (for example, a circle) or open with distinct endpoints (for example, a wavy line). Paths can have two types of anchor points: corner points and smooth points. At a corner point the path abruptly changes direction. At a smooth point, path segments are connected as a continuous curve. This system for changing the direction of the lines is called Bézier curves. The shape of the curve is defined by invisible points in the drawing. In general straight segments are drawn by clicking with the drawing tool (the pen), moving the mouse and clicking on a new point, and so on. Smooth, curved segments are created by clicking with the mouse and keeping the mouse button pressed while you adjust the shape of the curve. This shape can be modified later as desired by moving the anchor points.

The straight sections can be connected with curved segments. The outline of a path is usually called a stroke. A colour or gradient applied to the interior of an open or closed path is called a fill. A stroke can have weight (line thickness), colour and a solid or dashed line. After creating a path or shape you can edit its stroke and fill characteristics.

BÉZIER CURVES

Bézier curves is the name of a system developed around the 1960s for technical drawing in aircraft and car design. They are named after the French engineer Pierre Bézier, who used them in the design of different parts of car bodies during the years he worked at Renault. He devised a method of mathematical description of the curves that started to be successfully used in CAD programs (Computer Aided Design). This was publicised for the first time in 1962. The method was subsequently improved by Paul de Casteljau using the algorithm named after him. This is a numerically stable method for evaluating Bézier curves.

COMPARISON OF BITMAP IMAGES AND VECTOR GRAPHICS

BITMAPS	Formed by points, called pixels, arranged in a grid.	When a bitmap image is edited, the pixels that form it are changed.	Bitmap images are resolution-dependent, i.e. the information that forms them is fixed in a grid that has a specific size.	When an element in a bitmap is enlarged, the pixels are redistributed in the grid, which can cause uneven edges.	Bitmap images tend to take up a fairly substantial memory space. Although image compressors do exist, the files are usually quite large.
VECTOR GRAPH	Represent images using lines and curves, called vectors, including information regarding colour and positioning.	When a vector image is edited, the properties of the lines and curves describing its shape are changed.	Vector images are resolution-independent, which means they can be moved, resized, reshaped or their colour may be changed without degrading the image quality. Drawings may be scaled without any loss of information.	Changes in the size of vector images do not affect the image quality. The relationships and positions of the geometric elements that form them are mathematically reorganised.	Vector images allow designs to be stored in compact and small files.

Vector drawing can also be used in publishing texts, in multimedia and in the creation of 3D scenes. Virtually all 3D modelling programs use techniques that generate 2D vector graphics. There are also other kinds of more sophisticated tools which include actions on closed objects, such as grouping or welding, combining, intersecting and differentiating. Depending on the specific case, vector images may require less disc space than a bitmap. Some vector-based applications allow animation. This can be created simply through basic actions such as movement or rotation and does not require the storage of large amounts of data, so that the final files are still small and easily managed.

THE BÉZIER METHOD IN POSTSCRIPT
The inventors of PostScript, the language that facilitated the development of high-quality printing systems, adopted the Bézier method for generating the codes of the curves and paths. The PostScript language continues to be widely used and has become a universal quality standard, hence the vector design programs like Adobe Illustrator (AI), Macromedia's FreeHand (FH) which has been discontinued, CorelDRAW (CDR) – three of the most important vector drawing programs – include it in their features.

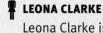

1 *Deco Dolly*. © Leone Clarke.
Vector drawing from a pencil sketch.

2 *Batgirl*. © Leone Clarke.
Mixed media.

3 *Bouffanties*. © Leone Clarke.
Vector drawing from a pencil sketch.

4 *Lock Work Girl*. © Leone Clarke.
Vector drawing from a pencil sketch.
(Illustration published in the magazine *Curvy 5*).

5 *Cherry Blossom Moon*. © Leone Clarke.
Vector drawing from a pencil sketch.
Her work begins with hand sketches, which she scans to
vectorise them using Illustrator, which helps to give her
work its characteristic effect. The artist herself tells us:
'I'm always drawing, I can't stop sketching with my
pencils and brushes.'

LEONA CLARKE

Leona Clarke is an illustrator based in London. She started studying *Design for Communication* at Chelsea College, where she discovered vector illustration, although she tells us she has spent years working on and developing her personal work. Her work has been acclaimed in the last two years, with her contributions to international magazines such as *Curvy 5* or *Amelia*.

She is particularly interested in retro periods. She says: 'I love Art Nouveau and Art Deco as well as the Japanese artist Wasarasa's printed textile designs.' Rooted in this source of inspiration, the artist creates a series of enigmatic illustrations, usually female figures to which she adds details, such as frames, landscape, or text, that reinforce the personality of the main figure.

www.leonaclarke.co.uk

ABOUT COLOUR IN DIGITAL GRAPHICS

We use colour models to describe the colours we see and work with in computer graphics. Each of the colour models, such as RGB (red, green, blue), CMYK (cyan, magenta, yellow, black) or HSB (hue, saturation, brightness), represents a different method for describing and classifying colour.

Colour models use numerical values to represent the visible spectrum of colour. A colour space is a variation of a colour model and has a specific range or 'gamut', of colours. For example, the RGB colour model has a number of colour spaces: Adobe RGB, sRGB and Apple RGB. While each of these spaces defines colour using the same three axes (R, G and B), their ranges are different.

When we work with colour in graphics, we are actually adjusting the numerical values in the file. It's easy to think of a colour as a number, but these numerical values are not absolute colours, they only have a colour meaning within the colour space of the device that is producing it.

Because each device has its own colour space, it can only reproduce the colours in its spectrum. When an image is moved from one device to another, the colours of the image may change because each device interprets the RGB or CMYK values according to its own colour space. For example, it is impossible for all the colours viewed in a monitor to be identically matched in a print from a desktop printer. A printer operates in a CMYK colour space while a monitor operates in an RGB colour space. Their ranges are different. Some colours produced by ink cannot be displayed on a monitor, and some colours that can be displayed on a monitor cannot be reproduced by using ink on paper.

THE RIGHT ENVIRONMENT

Your work environment influences how you see colour on your monitor and on the printed output. For best results, control the colours and light in your work environment by doing the following:

- View your documents in an environment that provides a consistent light level and colour temperature. For example, the colour characteristics of sunlight change throughout the day and alter the way colours appear on your screen, so keep blinds closed or work in a windowless room.

- You can also view printed documents using a D50 light box. View your document in a room with neutral-coloured walls and ceiling. A room's colour can affect the perception of both monitor colour and printed colour. The best colour for a viewing room is neutral gray. Also, the colour of your clothing reflecting off the glass of your monitor may affect the appearance of colours onscreen.

- Remove bright background colours from your monitor desktop. Busy patterns surrounding a document interfere with accurate colour perception. Set up your desktop to only display neutral grays.

- View document proofs in the real-world conditions under which your audience will see the final piece.

1

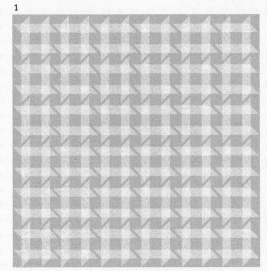

2

His work method starts with hand sketches
(drawing, cutting or painting) which he then finishes off
with his Macintosh (using various software).
His interests include recreating looks from the 1990s
or bizarre styles from the 1980s world of skateboarding.

1 *Lumbertooth*, © Breidholt Bobby.
All over print for Inmate Iceland. 2008.

2 *Boardwalk*. © Breidholt Bobby.
All over print for H&M worldwide. 2007.

3 Eye, © Breidholt Bobby.
Direct print for Inmate Iceland. 2008.

4 Brain, Bobby Breidholt ©.
Direct print for Inmate Iceland. 2006.

3

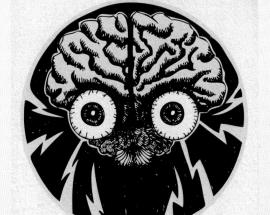

4

BOBBY BREIDHOLT

Bobby Breidholt was born in Reykjavik (Iceland)
in 1981, and obtained a Bachelor of Arts in
Graphic Design from The Icelandic Academy of
the Arts. He works as a freelance artist for
several textile and advertising companies. His
clients include companies such as H&M or
Inmate Iceland.

www.breidholt.com
flickr.com/breidholt

In her work she combines photographic images with vector drawing. She is currently developing a collection of prints with motifs from the architecture and cityscapes of Berlin, where she lives. She applies these black and white images of the city to all the items she designs.

Designs by Nadja Girod for the Smil collections. © Nadja Girod, 2007.

NADJA GIROD

Berlin-based designer Nadja Girod, creator of the Smil label consisting of bags and accessories that she designs herself with her own graphic motifs. They have limited editions and the range is widened each season, branching out to areas such as stationery or gifts. She has worked as a designer in a freelance capacity for several companies based in Spain, most notably for the women's lingerie chain Women'Secret. She distributes products under the Smil label in over 10 countries and also through her own website.

www.smil.biz
www.nadjagirod.com

COLOUR MANAGEMENT SYSTEMS

Colour-matching problems result from using various devices and software with different colour spaces. One solution is to have a system that interprets and translates colour accurately between devices. A Colour Management System (CMS) compares the colour space in which a colour was created with the colour space in which it will be printed, and makes the necessary adjustments to represent the colour as consistently as possible in different devices. The colour management system translates colour with the help of colour profiles (a profile is the mathematical description of a device's colour space). Colour management is not essential if the production process is tightly controlled for one medium only. For example, the user or their printing service provider can tailor CMYK images and specify colour values for a known, specific set of printing conditions.

The value of colour management increases when there are more variables in the production process. Colour management is recommended if you plan to reuse colour graphics for print and online media, use various kinds of devices within a single medium (such as different printing presses) or if you manage multiple workstations. A Colour Management System will be advantageous for any of the following objectives:

- Obtaining predictable and consistent colour output on multiple devices, such as colour separations, your desktop printer and your monitor.

- Accurately test a colour document on your screen, i.e. preview it by making it simulate a specific output device. Screen tests are subject to the limitations of monitor display and other factors such as room lighting conditions.

- Accurately evaluate and consistently incorporate colour graphics from many different sources if they also use colour management, and even in some cases if they don't.

- Sending colour documents to different output devices and media without having to manually adjust the colours in the documents or the original graphics. This is valuable when creating images that will be used both in print and online.

BASIC STEPS FOR PRODUCING CONSISTENT COLOUR
- Check with your production partners (if you have any) to ensure that all aspects of your colour management workflow integrate seamlessly with theirs.

- Calibrate and profile your monitor.

- Add colour profiles to your system for any input and output devices you plan to use, such as scanners and printers.

- Set up colour management in the applications you work with.

- Use colour management when printing and saving files.

The most popular software

There is no one technology for doing different kinds of design work. In fact, there are multiple programs, and consequently many ways of applying them.

We will start with the most basic systems related to Microsoft programs, from Paint, Office, which are normally installed in computers and are part of many primary and secondary schools' curricula, to Photoshop, Illustrator or CorelDRAW. However we will focus on the professional applications most widely used in the fashion industry.

The most popular software package in the fashion industry is undoubtedly Adobe's Creative Suite. It has resulted from Adobe's decision to combine all its professional programs (including Photoshop, Illustrator, InDesign, Acrobat, etc.), which previously could only be obtained separately, resulting in a lower purchase cost for the user and containing a very interesting set of tools for professional designers working in the various sectors of the industry. This ingenious combination of products has given Adobe good results in recent years, although the company also continues to sell its products on a stand-alone basis.

It is worth noting that there are many more 2D design programs that we have not included in our introduction, as we have given priority to the most common applications, used by the majority of designers and that are essential to know when competing in today's market. The subject of 3D design applied to the fashion industry is discussed in a whole section further on, which details new applications that satisfy an increasing demand in very specific sectors.

Domingo Ayala's graphics for his own collections use classic resources such as plain, bright colours and a naive-chic style, with allusion to vintage styles with a certain pop flair. He makes use of all the illustration technologies to produce his ideas, while staying faithful to the character of his original drawings.

Creations for the Domingo Ayala collection, Autumn / Winter 08-09.

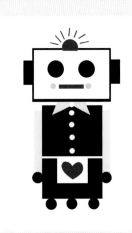

DOMINGO AYALA

Domingo Ayala's collections are divided into three sections. Firstly, clothing, which is mainly T-shirts, tops and sweaters, plus some dresses, and each garment is decorated with drawings, patches or embroidery also created by the designer. The second section includes handbags, purses and a few key rings. The third section has jewellery and vintage style gold chains combined with plastic and resin. These are original collections with clothing that is customised in great detail, young, casual, cheerful and colourful.

His prints make a direct reference to his graphic art, with their mythical tourists or wild flowers that have become the real personality of his brand: they are applied to all the elements of his collection, from direct screen prints to patches and zip pull tags.

www.domingoayala.com

ADOBE® PHOTOSHOP®

If we are going to highlight some of the programs most commonly used by designers we should start with Adobe Photoshop, perhaps one of the most ubiquitous in the creative industry. Nowadays the program has become an indispensable tool for enhancing all kinds of images.

The Adobe Photoshop (Ps) application is in the form of a paint and photography workshop that works on a canvas and is designed for retouching photographs and paintings made up of bitmap images, known in Photoshop as raster graphics. It was initially developed by the software company Adobe Systems for Apple computers, but was later adapted for the Windows operating system. Early versions of Photoshop worked in a one-layer bitmap space, to which a series of effects, texts, marks, and processing could be applied. Now it works with multiple layers. As the software has evolved various important improvements have been made, such as the incorporation of a multilayer work space (allowing transparency, previewing, etc.), inclusion of vector elements, advanced colour management and extensive typography editing, colour control and retouching, creative effects, the possibility of incorporating other companies' plugins and exporting to the Web, among others. The drawing tools allow vector shapes to be created and edited. Other tools and commands are used to transform and retouch images. When creating graphics on a computer, there is a distinction between painting and drawing. 'Painting' involves changing the colours of pixels using a painting tool. You can apply colours gradually, with soft edges and transitions, and manipulate individual pixels using powerful filter effects. However, once you apply a brush stroke, there is no simple way to select the whole stroke and move it to a new location in the image.

'Drawing', on the other hand, involves creating shapes that are defined as geometric objects (also called vector objects). For example, if you draw a circle using the Ellipse tool, the circle is defined by a specific radius, location, and colour. You can quickly select the entire circle and move it to a new location, or you can edit the outline of the circle to distort its shape. The latest versions of Adobe Photoshop software have added new features such as automatic alignment and merging of layers, which allows more complex compositions. The active filters add to the comprehensive set of non-destructive editing tools to offer greater flexibility, introducing a streamlined interface which is relatively intuitive to use.

Almost immediately after its launch, Photoshop became the world-standard photograph editing software, but it is also widely used in a multitude of disciplines in the design and photography fields, such as website design, bitmap image composition, digital modelling, photocomposition and video graphics and editing, and basically any activity that requires the editing of digital images. Adobe Photoshop has become market leader in raw image processing (editing of images taken with digital cameras), achieving incredible results in record time and optimum compatibility with over 150 camera models. Like all programs that work with bitmap images (i.e. rasterised images, also called pixmap or matrix images), Adobe Photoshop can be installed on Intel and PowerPC-based Macintosh computers and Microsoft Windows XP and Windows Vista systems. With the boom in digital photography in recent years, Photoshop has become increasingly popular outside professional fields, and is perhaps one of the most well-known software programs, or at least its name is familiar, for people starting to use it. Although Photoshop is mainly designed for photograph editing, it also can be used to create very good quality images, effects and graphics.

Photoshop layers allow us to fill any line drawing or scanned image with colour, texture or shading. Their great flexibility is ideal for designing and experimenting with different finishes and surfaces.

WORKING WITH LAYERS

Layers are basic properties of drawing and image editing programs. They are therefore an essential creative tool which it is vital to use to fully benefit from the program.

In Photoshop, a layer may contain information in a bitmap, vector texts or objects, masks, mix options, styles, opacity, adjustments, etc.

Some useful tips for working with layers in Photoshop are:

- Assign a meaningful name to each layer; you will be able to locate it more easily when you need it.

- Use layer groups to store specific layers or those common to a project.

- Group layers in subsets in each folder (the adjustments will be applied equally to all the layers of the same folder, unless you group some in a previous layer and preserve them from the adjustment).

- Colour-code the folders. You can assign colours to layers with the 'Layer properties' dialogue box.

- Reorder layer levels by dragging them in the 'Layers' palette. Link the layers by clicking on the link icon: move the elements to a layer and those on the linked layer will move with them (even if you drag them to another open file). This feature is useful if you have typographic adjustments in several layers that you need to move at once.

- Use layer groups to display different versions of a design to your clients.

- You can use the option 'Block transparency' in the 'Layers' palette to limit any edition of the part of the active layer that is not transparent. With the group clipping paths you can use a layer as a mask for one or more layer overlays. Use layer masks to crop parts of the background image. This conserves the whole image in case you need to make changes later. The 'Background' layer cannot be edited unless it is first changed to a separate layer (duplicate it or double-click on its icon in the 'Layers' palette). Remember that you will not be able to edit it if the document is in indexed colour mode.

- A text layer is automatically assigned the name of the text that you write in it. Leave this name unless several layers begin with the same words or characters.

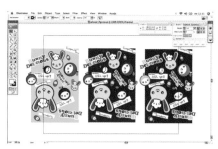

ADOBE® ILLUSTRATOR®

Adobe Illustrator is one of the programs that fashion professionals most commonly work with. It is used in practically all fashion design training, and is probably the most popular program in most professional fashion and design schools. Sophisticated illustrations can be created using Adobe Illustrator software, for virtually any medium (print, video, Web publishing and mobile devices).

Adobe Illustrator has, in a certain way, defined the language of contemporary graphic design through vector drawing. It features creative options, easier access to the tools and a great versatility for rapid production of graphics that are flexible and compatible with most current platforms. Adobe Illustrator has the sole and fundamental function of creating highly professional graphic-illustrative material, based on the production of mathematical objects called vectors. The extension of their files is .AI (Adobe Illustrator).Currently, it forms part of the Adobe Creative Suite family. Adobe Illustrator includes standard drawing tools, flexible colour controls, and professional type controls, which are essential for capturing our initial ideas and freely experimenting with them to obtain a definitive and professional result.

The latest versions of the program include significant improvements in optimisation of resources and the time required for the work. Among the tools that have been updated in the latest version, there are new controls for vector drawing, like the new Blob Brush, which allows you to sketch objects without worrying about overlapping, as it merges the paths in a single object. Transparency has been introduced to colour gradients, as well as the ability to use multiple art boards. This allows designers to work with areas of varying sizes as part of a single document without having to stack multiple pages.

The Adobe Creative Suite aims for full integration among its applications: all its components have a shared user interface design that gives greater workflow integration when using several of the applications, and making work simpler and faster.

Illustration based on a hand sketch
in the process of vectorisation.
© formatbrain, 2008.

Design of characters using
vector drawing.
© formatbrain, 2008.

FORMATBRAIN

Marcos Zerene is a 28-year-old Argentinian graphic designer, and the person behind formatbrain. He was born in Mendoza and studied at the Faculty of Arts and Design of the Universidad Nacional de Cuyo; he currently lives in Barcelona.

The sources of exploration, styles and influences for his work include illustration books and the Internet. The formatbrain technique combines hand drawing with digitalisation. Although he works vectorally on some characters, the majority only have digital adjustments made using a graphics tablet or programs such as Photoshop and Illustrator. Most of his characters arise from everyday life, inspired by a combination of streets, the Internet, television, cinema and the artist's own imagination.

His work has been disseminated on the Internet through the huge Flickr community. His creations include two paper toys for 100% Loading, exhibited at the Pixie Gallery in Japan and at PP@ART, Taipei 2007. He has also worked with cutmilkmagazine and for LeToy. Formatbrain's characters also reach the street through paste-ups and graffiti in cities such as Barcelona, Berlin, Amsterdam and Budapest.

http://www.flickr.com/people/formatbrain

You can use up to 100 artboards and display them in whatever way you like, overlapped, stacked or side by side. These boards can be exported as a single multipage PDF document or as a series of numbered pages. The Adobe Creative Suite's overall trend is towards greater automating of everyday tasks and working directly on the workspace, which makes interacting with tools and options easier. Adobe also aims for full integration among the package components. With new user interface similarity among the tools, work across Creative Suite components is homogeneous and virtually seamless. Adobe Illustrator is perfectly compatible with the latest hardware and software of Intel-based Macintosh computers and Microsoft Windows Vista systems. It is widely compatible with all the standard industry graphics file formats, including PDF, EPS, Photoshop (PSD), TIFF, GIF, JPEG, SWF, SVG, DWG, DXF, etc.

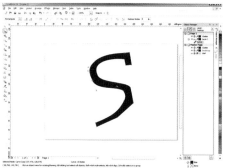

CORELDRAW GRAPHICS®

Although CorelDRAW is not widely used by the fashion industry, and neither is it on the curriculum of the principal schools, it offers adequate tools for professional work. Firstly, it can help us in photo editing (it enables retouching and enhancing speedily and accurately). It also includes intuitive applications for page layout design and vector drawing, offering enormous possibilities for professional designers or someone who wishes to obtain optimal results. CorelDRAW offers exclusive and highly practical tools for sketching fashion figures, diagrams for garment technical specification sheets and for the creation of textile prints, such as the interactive fill tool, the option of automatic vectorising including colour reduction, previewing of colour separations for textile screen printing, etc. It is worth highlighting two specific tools for the final design of these boards: the CorelDRAW interactive table, which allows you to create and import tables to achieve a structured design of text and graphics, and independent page layers that provide greater control and allow you to create individual page layouts in a multiple-page document.

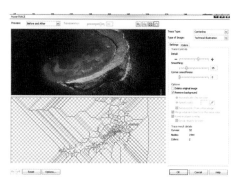

The latest version of the program is distributed as part of CorelDRAW® Graphics Suite X4, with precision tools, high file compatibility and high-quality content that help transform creative ideas into professional results. CorelDRAW Graphics Suite X4 provides all the graphics tools needed for:

- Illustration, with powerful vector tools
- Graphic design
- Editing and enhancing digital images
- Vectorisation of bitmap images

CorelDRAW Graphics Suite X4 also comes with additional applications and services, adapting to the new digital languages to help cover users' different requirements.

The Freehand program interface contains the necessary tools to develop any design work, combining the effectiveness of vector drawing with the ability to insert bitmap graphics in our workspace.

The drawing tools are very similar to those in other vector programs, which facilitates migration to other applications. In addition, formats such as .pdf or .eps allow us to display our designs using different software.

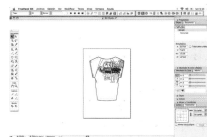

FREEHAND®

Freehand is another of the key programs. Over the last few decades it has unarguably been a standard reference point in design. FreeHand enables the creation of vector graphics to which any scale or print resolution can be applied. FreeHand MX can be used to create graphic illustrations or any other artwork with powerful design and colour control tools. The company that produced and distributed FreeHand was acquired by Adobe, since which time important changes are taking place in the industry. While we recognise FreeHand has a loyal customer base, we encourage users try the new Adobe Illustrator CS3 which is compatible with both PowerPC and Intel-based Macs and Microsoft Windows XP and Windows Vista.

No updates have been produced for Freehand for several years, and Adobe does not appear to have the intention of developing new features or supporting Intel-based Macs and Windows Vista. Macromedia FreeHand MX is a vector drawing application. Using FreeHand, vector graphics can be created that are scalable and printable at any resolution without losing detail and sharpness. You can use FreeHand MX to create and print web illustrations, such as logos and advertisements. You can also use FreeHand MX to turn your artwork into Macromedia Flash animations. The FreeHand user interface contains a workspace and a tool panel similar to other Macromedia products such as Macromedia Dreamweaver, Fireworks and Flash, providing a truly integrated print and web solution. Now documents can be viewed and tested in a Macromedia Flash playback window without leaving the FreeHand environment. FreeHand is an application that enables you to draw vector graphics. Vector graphics are resolution-independent: graphics can be scaled to any size and printed on an output device at any resolution without losing detail or sharpness of the image.

Fashion Illustration

Following its golden age of glamour of the 1940s and 1950s, fashion illustration suffered decades of media ostracism. Now it once again occupies a position of honour.

Fashion illustration has returned to the heart of the professional arena with new airs, enormous figures and new techniques of expression. The fashion illustration market continues to grow, encompassing magazines, books, catalogues, advertising, television, etc. The increasing demand encourages young talent to seek acclaim and drive their careers forward. The most notable aspect of the work of the new generations of artists is the variety of methods they use, and their intensive use of mixed media techniques. A drawing done with a pencil or paintbrush can be worked on with digital techniques that enable it to be completed with a greater wealth of graphics, details or colour, or to be manipulated as a vector drawing. This use of technology does not in any way reduce the creativity and originality of the designs, which continue to capture the artist's personality. With this aim, software applications have been adapted to the changing needs of young artists and new potential has been incorporated to the programs, improving the final result of the work.

Her creations mix work with real volumes on paper that are photographed and digitalised, with plain colour silhouettes, creating very harmonious schematic full figures. The techniques she develops unmistakably define her own creative personality.

Untitled. © 2007 Alexandra Zaharov.
Russia. Mixed media.
Illustrations for the magazine *Fashion Collection*.

ALEXANDRA ZAHAROVA

This artist lives and works in Moscow, where she collaborates with fashion agencies and media. Her work demonstrates young artists' tremendous creative potential. Her work is the result of well-planned stages of work that have earned her a niche in the current creative context.

www.flickr.com/photos/25436168@No8

AUTOMATIC LAYER ALIGNMENT
The 'Auto-align layers' command lets you automatically align layers based on similar content in different layers, such as corners and edges. The tool lets you assign one layer as a reference layer, or lets the Photoshop program automatically choose the reference layer. Other layers are then aligned to the reference layer so that matching content overlays itself. This method facilitates the replacement or removal of parts of images that have the same background, or images with overlapping content.

NEW ADOBE® PHOTOSHOP® ILLUSTRATION TOOLS

The latest versions of Adobe Photoshop optimise the work of many fashion illustrators, incorporating new tools to make selections more quickly and define edges. With the new features you can loosely draw on an image area and the quick selection tool automatically completes the selection for you. Your selection can be refined using the simple sliders. Another development contained in the latest versions of Adobe Photoshop are intelligent filters, which allow us to add, adjust and remove filters from an image without having to resave the image or start over again to preserve quality. Regarding work in layers – which comprise the final image – you can now automatically align Photoshop layers or images based on similar content. The auto-align layers command quickly analyses details and moves, rotates or warps layers to align them perfectly.

WAYS OF DRAWING

When you work with the shape or pen tools, you can draw in three different modes. You can choose a mode by selecting an icon from the options bar when you have a shape or pen tool selected.

- Shape layers: creates a shape on a separate layer. You can use either the shape tools or the pen tools to create shape layers. Shape layers are easily moved, resized, aligned and distributed. You can choose to draw multiple shapes on a layer. A shape layer consists of a fill layer that defines the shape colour and a linked vector mask that defines the shape outline. The outline of a shape is a path, which appears in the 'Paths' palette.

- Paths: draws a work path on the current layer that you can then later use to make a selection, create a vector mask, or fill and stroke with colour to create raster graphics (much as you would using a painting tool). A work path is temporary unless you save it. Paths appear in the Paths palette.

- Fill Pixels: paints directly on a layer – much as a painting tool does. When you work in this mode, you're creating raster images – not vector graphics. You work with the shapes you paint just as you do with any raster image. Only the shape tools work in this mode

1 *My legs love Paris.* © 2007 Jacklyn Laryea.
Mixed media: pencil, Adobe Illustrator CS3,
Abobe Photoshop cs3.

2 *According to fashion.* © 2007 Jacklyn Laryea.
Mixed media: pencil, Adobe Illustrator CS3,
Abobe Photoshop cs3.

3 *Jagvil: think fashion.* © 2008 Jacklyn Laryea.
Mixed media: pencil, Adobe Illustrator CS3, Adobe
Photoshop cs3.

4 *Ispy.* © 2007 Jacklyn Laryea.
Mixed media: pencil, Adobe Illustrator CS3,
Adobe Photoshop cs3.

Jacklyn develops hand sketches and then transforms
them with Photoshop and Illustrator into final artwork.
She always tries to highlight the personal and
emotional features of the initial sketch, looking for
elements of human 'imperfection' in her
vector work.

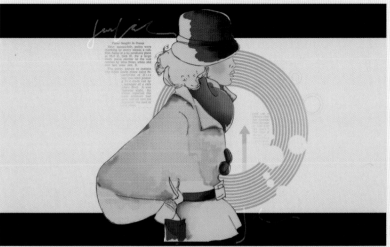

JACKLYN LARYEA
She began her artistic career when she was
just 17. She says: 'In those years new
computing applications and vector images
began to replace photography as the only
means of representation'. Jacklyn studied Fine
Arts, but soon discovered in digital illustration
'the work mode of her generation'.

Her work is, in a nutshell, a good example
of simplicity and harmony found in
illustrations that are bursting with personality
and dynamism. The artist says that her
ultimate goal, rather than seeking references
in the work of world-famous artists, is to
experiment with her own work. At present,
Jacklyn heads up her own design, illustration
and multimedia studio, from which she
continues to develop her more creative and
professional work.

www.jackielaryea.com

ADOBE® ILLUSTRATOR® SOLUTIONS FOR ILLUSTRATORS

The potential of vector drawing has increased with additions to programs which aim to complete them and optimise results. The new versions of Adobe Illustrator offer easier and more flexible anchor point selection, and a new 'Eraser' tool which helps enormously to create artwork efficiently and intuitively. This new tool allows us to erase pixels in the same way as in Photoshop, enjoying complete control over the width, shape and smoothness of the erasure.

Another tool that deserves a special mention for fashion designers is 'Live Colour'. If we start with a freehand sketch we can 'trace it' in a vector drawing, for example, to create artwork based on a pencil sketch drawn on paper or on a raster image saved in another program. The easiest way to trace artwork is to open or place a file in Illustrator and automatically trace the artwork with the 'Live Trace' command. You can control the level of detail and how the tracing is filled. When you are satisfied with the result, you can convert the tracing to vector paths or a live trace object. You can also select any artwork and interactively edit colours to immediately see results. Using the Colour Guide panel you can quickly choose tints, shades or harmonious colour combinations. For more complicated work (with a lot of detail or many elements), the latest versions of Adobe Illustrator incorporate the 'Isolation mode', for editing a group of objects without affecting other parts of your illustrations. This allows objects that are difficult to find to be easily selected without having to reorder, nor manually lock or hide objects.

THE 'PENCIL' TOOL

It is particularly useful for direct, spontaneous drawing, quick sketches and giving a hand-drawn look to any digital representation with the advantage that once the drawing is done, it can be modified with computer tools. As you draw with the 'Pencil' tool, anchor points are set down which can be adjusted once the path is completed. The number of anchor points is determined by the length and complexity of the path and by the tolerance settings of the 'Pencil tool preferences' dialogue box. These settings control how sensitive the Pencil tool is to the movement of your mouse or graphics-tablet stylus.

CONVERT A PHOTOGRAPHIC IMAGE TO A VECTOR DRAWING

Vectorisation is the conversion of a rasterised graphic (or bitmap) into a vector drawing. This process can either be done manually, making a copy of the raster image, or using a specific tool, such as Adobe Illustrator's 'Live Trace'. A live trace object is formed by two components, the original image and the trace result (which is the trace of the drawing). Although by default only the trace result is visible, you have the option of changing the way the original image and the trace result are displayed on screen according to your needs.

1

2

3

The main tool used in her work is Adobe Illustrator. With it she brings new dimensions to vector drawing. Her work stands out for its highly creative nature. She uses Adobe Illustrator's potential to the full – more than a tool it becomes an extension of the artist's personality. Her illustrations represent the spirit (and fashion) of her time: the street, television and celebrities are the basis of her work.

1 *Self-portrait*. Vector drawing, 2007
© Shirleymoon.

2 *Portrait of Jimmy Choo*. Vector drawing, 2007
© Shirleymoon. Work from the exhibition *Shine!* 2007 organised by the British Council.

3 *Self-portrait*. Vector drawing, 2007
© Shirleymoon. Work from the exhibition *Shine!* 2007 organised by the British Council.

 SHIRLEYMOON

Shirley Moon is an illustrator from Hong Kong who lives and works in London. After graduating from London's Middlesex University she began working as an freelance professional illustrator. She says: 'I was always attracted to vector illustration. My biggest influence is without doubt the work of the Airside Studio in London' (www.airside.co.uk). Her early work consisted of a series of self-portraits that she began to exhibit while she was completing her training. Subsequently the British Council invited her to participate in the international contest *Shine!* International Student Award & Exhibition 2007.

www.shirleymoon.com
www.thechipfactory.co.uk

The images we show of Peter Wilson's work represent the perfection of his working system: layering hand drawn illustrations that little by little are filled with colour and form thanks to the design application that he uses (Photoshop). He divides his work into layered groups of figures, garments and depths, in this way he is able to work in each of these autonomous forms.

All the images, 2008, Mixed technique.
©Peter Wilson.

 PETER WILSON

He perfectly combines manual sketching with the creative possibilities of digital tools. His work retains the feeling of a sketch but at the same time he adds a series of textures and digital brush strokes to the original scanned drawing that make the final artwork richer. His technical process openly reveals the method he follows in his work. In his case, the mixed media technique is essential to give the final representation a strong personality. Peter Wilson carries out his work in urban art under the name goonism. The artist's work is completed by stickers, graffiti and other artistic expressions of an urban nature.

goonism@yahoo.co.uk

DISSEMINATING ILLUSTRATIONS ON THE INTERNET

The use of digital media is equally as important for the illustrations to be disseminated in the global market, i.e. making the work available to any user around the globe. In fact, we are familiar with many designers' work due to them having entrusted their work to digital media such as Myspace, Flickr, blogs or their own personal websites (discussed earlier in this book), enabling the work to acquire a global scope that is fundamental for developing any project and becoming known professionally. In this way, today's fashion illustrator can receive orders in line with their specific style from any region or country in the world.

FTP (File Transfer Protocol) SPACE

A FTP server is a special program that runs on a server normally connected to the Internet (although it may be connected to other networks -LAN, MAN-) which, as its name suggests, is for transferring files from your hard disc to a server. They are very useful for sending large format files anywhere in the world. Its purpose is to enable data movement between different servers or computers. FTP servers can be used either as a server for illustrators and their clients to share image files or as a backup (security copy) of important files that a company may have.

In his illustrations he skilfully combines very personalised hand sketches with effects and finishes from digital platforms. Photoshop's retouching and conversion features allow him to modify the images and take a great variety of steps to improve composition, correct distortions or defects, creatively modify elements of the image, add or remove elements and focus, blur or combine several images in a panorama.

Glasses. Mixed media.
© Danny Roberts.

DANNY ROBERTS

After finishing his studies in Fashion Illustration at the Academy of Art University of San Francisco, he began his career working as a freelance artist for fashion media. His work ranges from portraits of models and celebrities to fashion features for written publications. He tells us he is strongly attracted by the illustrations he finds in old books or in Krzysztof Kieslowski films, and he doesn't hesitate to search for this effect in his work.

Undeniably, Danny Roberts's work defines to perfection the enormous possibilities that the industry offers young talent – work to be contemplated and admired.

www.iqons.com/danny+roberts

He doesn't hesitate to mix techniques, media or materials, from digital photography and images obtained from the Internet to hand drawings and digital sketches. The new tools, which allow him to experiment with all kinds of media, are key to his creative development. He tells us that he scans all the material to be able to mount his compositions using different Photoshop layers. In fact, he uses some elements in other work, in this way defining his own expressive language.

All images. *Maniquí*. 2007, Mixed media.
© Raül Vázquez.

RAUL VAZQUEZ

Raul Vázquez is a Spanish artist who currently works as a fashion illustrator and designer. He collaborates with different media and in 2007 was invited to participate with his artwork in the presentation of the fashion festival 080 Barcelona. He defines his work method as follows: 'I love the world of fashion, art and illustration. In each creative process I try to present an idea and develop it. Turn it around, play with it, enjoy it. For that reason I don't limit myself from using any available tools which can help me to paint or illustrate my prints.' His interests revolve around 'fashion, love and sexual desire' and he tries to depict these themes throughout his work.

He conceives work in the fashion industry as a social engine, art linked to design, the communication of concepts and ideas and the plurality of themes; in short, a collage of ideas that he attempts to express in his work.

www.myspace.com/raul_vazquez

This illustrator uses fashion magazine clippings to work with the eye area in her illustrations.

Fashion style meets hair style.
2007, mixed media (series of three illustrations for the client underwired, USA).
© Kerstin Wacker.

KERSTIN WACKER

Fashion design is Kerstin Friedericke Wacker's main line of work. She is currently based in Berlin although she has worked in Hong Kong, Istanbul and also in Paris, where she was a fashion illustrator for *Printemps* department stores. In 2004 she started in her new studio, wacker eins! and began her work as a freelance fashion illustrator for international clients, contributing to fashion magazines and companies. Part of her work can be seen in the winter 09 collection for the company Custo Barcelona. Concerning her illustrations she tells us: 'I want to create characters with strong personalities, self-confident and beautiful; I use fashion to emphasise their attitudes.'

www.wacker1.com

In her illustrations she combines hand sketches with digital techniques.

Horse Race. 2007, mixed media.
(collage for the client Fandenrot. Germany).
© Kerstin Wacker

This illustration combines hand drawing, digital techniques and the application of magazine clippings.

Spring Wake. 2008, mixed media.
© Kerstin Wacker.

Kerstin's work perfectly combines hand sketches (pencils and paint brushes) with digital backgrounds or elements. Photoshop is her great ally for this kind of work. In particular, for creating this kind of association between various elements, mask layers are an essential feature. Masks allow you to make areas of one or more images transparent, which means several elements can be blended together in a very subtle way, creating illustrations of a very high standard and level of detail.

This tool has the advantage that when the layer mask is applied, pixels are not removed from the image but are only hidden, which means that you can subsequently edit and reveal the areas that have been hidden.

In theory, layer masks are greyscale images that show what is defined in white and hide what is painted in black. They allow a wide range of shades of grey which in turn, become levels of transparency.

La Plage. 2008, mixed media.
© Kerstin Wacker.

Development of prints and direct prints

In the last few decades, new technologies have had a huge impact on the design of prints and direct prints for the textile industry.

Firstly, they have allowed people working in other areas of design (graphics, illustration, etc.) to take part in creative fashion projects. Secondly, an entire annex industry of digital textile printing has been built up that allows new design proposals to be taken on more easily, minimising production times. Although it's true that the price of digital printing can be a constraint for some designers, it is also true that we will soon see prices stabilise in a parallel way to the growth of their potential market. In this section we will look at the potential of both textile design using digital techniques and of its subsequent development into production. Within print design there are many examples of the use of new computing applications. If you aim for a realistic or photographic effect, it is advisable to use bitmap images. In recent decades, some designers who opt for combining work done by hand with digital techniques (creating very personalised work) have achieved wide market acceptance (the success of the result depends on the resolution and the printing technique used).

Similarly, we find designers who are using vector images for their work applied to the design of prints and direct prints. These vector files normally use a direct colour separation, which facilitates their final printing. The size and shape of the vector files can be modified without affecting their resolution or sharpness, greatly facilitating their application to garments or accessories.

Chris Gray's work is characterised by an enormous expressiveness in the use of lines and the mass of colour. In the majority of his work he uses vector graphics to create his animes or humanised forms. The use of contrasting and defined colours helps him to create his desired effects.

Pictures from the collection *30 shirts / 30 days* © Chris Gray.

Proposal submitted by Chris Gray for the DESIGN-A-TRUCK CONTEST. Freitag 2008.

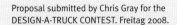

CHRIS GRAY

A University of Salford graduate, he has worked with several London studios including Love Creative, with clients such as BBC, Christian Aid, PlayStation or Dr. Martens. One of his most recent projects, *30 shirts / 30 days*, has led him to design a T-shirt for every day of the month, from which we show some examples.

www.weshallsee.co.uk

Any innovation in the world of graphic design is immediately transferred to printing. Design is evolving with the new line-drawing or pixel tools, graphic or artistic trends, 3D graphics, new filters, textures and finishes. Many of these garments have sprung out from their usual context to reach museums, art galleries or interactive spaces. The design of prints and direct prints has been greatly enriched with the contribution from professionals from different areas (graphic design, painting, illustration, photography, etc.). The work opportunities provided by the new design and communication media are multiplied both geographically (we can work on international projects from any geographical location) and operationally (nowadays designers have a wide variety of tools at their disposal to apply). Furthermore, the market constantly demands innovation and generates this continual search for interdisciplinary activity that is necessary to develop innovative and unexpected designs.

USING A GRAPHICS TABLET

A graphics tablet or digitiser consists of a flat surface upon which the user can draw an image using a stylus (pen) that comes with the tablet. The current styli have a pressure-sensitive tip capable of recognising several levels, just like a graphite pencil. The graphics tablet is a peripheral element which has two basic functions: it allows the user to introduce hand or graphic drawings and make notes or point to the objects on the screen. Logically, the image appears on the computer screen not on the tablet. Graphics tablets have numerous features that make them the perfect tool for drawing directly on the computer. Because of their stylus-based interface and ability to detect pressure, tilt and other attributes of the stylus and its interaction with the tablet, graphic tablets are widely used to create computer graphics, especially two-dimensional computer graphics. Indeed, many graphics packages (e.g. Corel Painter, Photoshop and others) are able to make use of the pressure, stylus tilt and rotation by modifying the brush size, shape, opacity, colour, or other attributes based on data received from the graphics tablet. Some users find these more intuitive than a mouse, as the position of the stylus on the tablet corresponds to the location of the pointer on the graphical user interface shown on the computer screen. In the same way as with a traditional pencil, many modern styli even include an eraser at the top of the stylus, and an additional electric circuit that is used

The prints and direct prints that Mike Perry designs have evolved along with his parallel line of visual arts (he has contributed to numerous books and graphics magazines). His creations range from typography work to motifs which define his creative language. Four examples of direct prints designs for T-shirts. © Mike Perry.

when using the eraser, usually similar or identical to the one used for the tip. The eraser is also pressure-sensitive. In this way, you can delete various layers of colour from the picture depending on the pressure applied or it may be assigned other functions such as deleting different brushes or other characteristics. The digitiser tablets at the lower end of the range usually detect 256 levels of pressure; a normal tablet detects 512 levels, while a professional-range tablet may be able to detect 1,024 levels of pressure. Digitiser tablets are available in various sizes and prices: A6 size are the most economical, A3 size are much more expensive. The current digitiser tablets usually connect to a USB interface, some users who want avoid having too many cables around their computer transfer data to the computer via Bluetooth, and others use wireless links.

MICHAEL PERRY

He sends us his designs for T-shirts and sweatshirts from his studio in Brooklyn, New York. His graphic work also includes contributions to books and magazines as well as multidisciplinary projects. His clients include *New York Times Magazine, Dwell Magazine, Microsoft Zune, Urban Outfitters, eMusic or Zoo York*. His creations have been highly acclaimed in specialised publications such as *Step Magazine* or *Computer Arts Projects Magazine*. In 2008 he received *Print Magazines'* New Visual Artist award. In August 2008 he presented his first solo exhibition entitled *The Place between Time and Space*.

www.midwestisbest.com

Their representations are as varied as their creators, but their productions are dominated by a sense of humour and, above all, the ironic language full of messages for the audience and bursting with elements of contemporary iconography.

Direct printing T-shirt designs for the Threadless label.
© Threadless

THREADLESS

A project based on the collaboration of graphic designers from around the world, which creates printed T-shirts for the younger market. Designers include the Frenchman Jean-Sébastien Deheeger, the British designer Stuart Colebrook and Dustin Amery Hostetler from the US, although currently the brand has more than 30 staff involved in printing.

The core of the brand image is undoubtedly its website, which promotes, communicates and sells online products and also encourages social participation and communication between staff and Internet users (features of Web 2.0).

www.threadless.com

SCREENPRINTING

Screenprinting is a very popular printing system, especially in the textiles industry, as it can work with the most varied of surfaces: metals, plastics, glass, wood, cloth, etc. Fabric printing, particularly on T-shirts, is perhaps one of its best-known applications. Using screenprinting, attractive and innovative designs can be developed, and it is even relatively easy to customise a design for promotions or limited editions.

Screenprinting works by allowing the ink to pass when the woven mesh or stencil is pressed with a wide rubber spatula or 'squeegee'. This mesh may be made of metal or synthetic threads, which are finely woven. A light-sensitive substance is spread on this mesh. This is how the model is constructed using solarisation photographic techniques, forming a screen that lets the ink pass in those areas that have been in contact with the light, and blocking the mesh in the areas where this substance has not been released. With this system a significantly thick layer of ink is deposited – at least in comparison with other methods – so that the printed image is long-lasting, which is necessary for items of clothing that will inevitably undergo a series of washes and wear over time.

FEATURED PRODUCT: THE T-SHIRT

If there is one fashion item that takes centre stage in terms of graphics work for the textile industry, it is the printed T-shirt. Many people call it the fetish garment of our casual-street culture, with thousands of labels whose sole business is to produce T-shirt designs and both physical and online sales outlets that pay homage to this garment. From a product viewpoint, the impact of the market is such that a few decades ago the 'limited series' T-shirt business began, collectors' items with exclusive distribution and few copies (like artwork, prints, photographs, etc.). Within this commercial whirlwind various businesses are beginning to stand out for their development of T-shirts designed with the collaboration of illustrators, graffiti artists, well-known artists, bands, celebrities or renowned architects, etc.; icons of our time for the younger generation, which reflect the artistic preoccupations of young contemporary designers.

Both traditional points of sale (that create spaces for displaying and selling these designs) and new online platforms give the sector a leading role. One of the greatest factors in the success of online sales services lies in their universality of shapes and sizes. In fact, sales points on the Internet have multiplied in number, from large distributors with a wide range to mini-businesses created by a designer who is responsible for everything: product design, the website and managing sales and production. This gives rise to the individual creation of ultra-personalised projects with a strong brand image and a small budget for their execution.

Their first collection includes the participation of Stephanie (Sydney), Michael Gillette (San Francisco), Christina Kouropyrou (London), Saksi (Paris) and Cesc (Barcelona). The artwork selected for each collection are included in the clothing and on the packaging, which, as already mentioned, simulates a record sleeve.

© Teachheart.

The label regularly organises contests to search for new collaborators interested in participating in the project. The winning designs are put into production, and there is also a money prize for the winners.

T-shirts from the first collection of the label thGallery for Teachheart.
© Teachheart.

TEACHHEART

This young company, at the forefront of the Paris artscene, offers a collection of T-shirts with the collaboration of different artists under the label thGallery, distributed as limited series and packaged in sleeves that mimic record sleeves, customised by the same designer.

Each piece is unique and is made and stamped by its designer. The label is responsible for complying with all the environmental controls in the production of these exquisite pieces, raised to the category of works of art.

In their website, not only can you read about the label's projects, but also obtain information about their contests, news, and shop in the online sales section.

www.teach-heart.com
www.thgallery.fr

DIGITAL PRINTING

Digital printing techniques have been on the market for several years. They started being used professionally in relation to the design of prototypes or mini-collections. Currently, many designers have opted for this technique due to the improvement in its quality and price and, above all, the optimisation of production in terms both of time and fabric. Whilst it cannot be said that digital printing will eliminate traditional techniques from the market, it does seem that it has created an important niche for itself in the contemporary scene.

Analogue printing uses a master, the traditional manual printing frames. The boards are screens or plates with the different print colours. Although they can be prepared by digital techniques, they eventually become an analogue master from which copies are made. It is necessary to use several screens, one for each colour.

Engraving the screens is very costly: more than half the total production time is used in engraving and preparing samples. Therefore, the printer runs a great risk and must be very clear on the profitability of an item before engraving screens. In our experience, only between 40% and 60% of new designs generate enough orders to cover the costs incurred.

The current trend in textiles is the production of a growing number of original and exclusive designs, which require a rapid response. Retailers do not want to keep a large inventory, which results in the reduction of the lengths of cloth printed per design and colourway. The average length printed in Europe is 1,000 metres per colourway.

Working with shorter batch lengths means that the machine downtime increases, as it is necessary to clean, change the screens and the ink to start processing another design. For this reason the volume of orders covers less and less of the cost of the samples. The ideal way to reduce the costs of traditional printing and the risks implicit in the creation of a collection is to eliminate the screens from the sample and/or production process. Various market studies conclude that application of digital printing to the preparation of samples along with the production of short print runs for finished products end will grow significantly in the next few years. With digital printing the upfront costs are removed, thus only the final production is paid for per metre.

PRINT ITEM

In digital printing, unlike with photography, the print point size does not increase with the size of the image. It depends on the output resolution of the printer and on the drop size selected at the time of printing. However, what is possible is that if we enlarge a bitmap image, the size of the pixels increases, and in this case some larger points are visible that produce the unwanted 'jaggies' effect of stair-like lines.

PRODUCTION THROUGH DIGITAL TEXTILE PRINTING

Nowadays digital technology is used for the production not only of samples but also of usable products. One of the disadvantages of the application of this new technology is the speed of production, which is still very slow compared to traditional printing.

Despite this disadvantage, many new markets are being developed where digital technology provides a unique solution that cannot be obtained using conventional technology (exclusive fashion, silk kimonos with the pattern printed in a way that the design remains continuous, etc.).

The advantages of digital printing are:

- Instant change of design, without downtime.
- Samples and production use the same technology.
- No need for engraving of screens.
- Less use of dyes and chemical products. More ecologically sound.
- Requires less labour.
- Minimises stocks.
- Reduces delivery time (to a point).
- Possibility of photo-realism with precision and fine detail.
- There is no additional cost for the addition of a greater number of colours.

Digital printing techniques can be applied to all kinds of fabrics, from the finest to the thickest; with more or less dimensional stability (which is determined by the lightness or elasticity of the fabric, i.e. its ability to deform), even leather pieces, cut patterns or tailored garments. There are machines for all needs. It is therefore very important to define exactly what you want to obtain from the digital printing and to select the printer that can best meet your expectations.

Hotel Lobby, 2008.
Client: Custo Barcelona print for Summer 09 collection.
Mixed media: a mixture of inks.
Pantone and Photoshop techniques.
© Kerstin Wackerwww.wacker1.com

Miami, 2008. Printing for the Custo Barcelona Summer 09 collection. Custo Barcelona is one of the leading companies on the professional scene in the use of prints and applications developed with digital techniques. Their illustrations normally have so many shades of colour and details that digital printing techniques have yielded excellent results in their garments.
© Kerstin Wacker.www.wacker1.com

PRINT FILES

The print files are the digital files (photographs, illustrations, drawings, scanned pictures) we give to the printer to produce the particular print. The result of the work depends on these print files.

For this reason, the following points are essential:

- The use of appropriate creative software.

- The correct pixel size (resolution) of the image, which takes into account the final size to be printed and the type of substrate.

- The quality of the colour of photographic images.

TYPES OF INK

There are currently two types of special ink developed for use in digital textile printing: inks based on soluble textiles dyes and inks based on pigments.

In the first group we have:

- Reactive dye ink, used principally for cotton and cellulose fibres.
- Disperse dye ink, used for polyester both directly and through transfer printing.
- Acid dye ink, used for wool, silk and polyamide fabrics.

The second group comprises pigment-based inks. The duration and stability of the colours obtained in digital printing depends on the substrate of the colour base or binding agent (which may be water, glue, PVC, etc.), on the inks and on the processing carried out before and after, such as fixing, washing and drying. These pigment-based inks for digital printing of textiles are in great demand in the market. The advantage of these inks is that they can print on any type of fabric, regardless of its composition. They are adhered to any fabric regardless of the type of material or its texture using a binding agent (the substance that we add to the colour so that it adheres to the fabric). The solidity of the results is acceptable, as well as the intensity of the colours obtained. The solidity determines the durability of the colour after washing. When using pigment-based inks, it is possible to work without preparing the fabric. However, it is advisable to do this prior preparation, which involves removing the sizing (the resin on the surface of fabric), so that the weave of the fabric is open and allows the colour to be absorbed. The ink must preferably have a low viscosity for the header to work without the printhead clogging. Working with pigments, after polymerisation, the degree of solidity is not affected by the prior preparation of the fabric. When we use inks for transfer printing it is not necessary to coat the fabric as we use special transfer paper. When we make a transfer print we are applying a tracing on the fabric with the help of heat. This printing method comprises two steps: firstly the printer has to pass the desired image to the transfer paper using special heat transfer inks, secondly heat is applied to the previously inked transfer paper by pressure applied with an iron to fix the image on the fabric. Printing using this kind of transfer technique does not require bulky equipment, making it the ideal tool for small businesses that offer exclusive and customised clothing.

When doing direct printing, using textile dye-based inks specific to each fibre, we should note that the ink only contains the dye. If we want the fabric to have the same solidity properties as conventional printing, all the auxiliary substances required to fix the dye to the fibre must be previously added to the fabric. If you have not removed the sizing correctly and if the fabric is not ready to receive the print, the colours that are applied on the surface won't be able to penetrate the fabric weave and solidity values will be very low, even zero, which means that the colour may be lost after a few washes.

Solutions for 2D garment design

Over the course of history, the need to communicate with drawings led to two distinct forms of representation – artistic drawing and technical drawing. While the former tries to communicate ideas and feelings, based on suggestion and interpretation, stimulating the viewer's imagination, technical drawing is aimed at the geometrical and mathematical representation of objects.

In the field of fashion design, the objectives of artistic and technical drawing converge. This is due to the use of computers in technical drawing, which although they represent the true size and shape of objects, are also highly suggestive for the viewer. However, it is important to note that this does not mean that fashion designers do not use artistic design. In fact, most of them do, especially in the first phase of the overall process. Drawing is an exercise in abstraction of the human spirit that allows the appearance of a shape to be defined, given that the human eye only perceives coloured masses of varying light intensity. Furthermore, drawing is the art of graphically representing objects that usually have three dimensions on a two-dimensional flat surface. However, new technologies are undeniably playing an important role in the design of products in the fashion industry. There is such an abundant choice that it is very difficult to synthesise all the information in a single chapter. Once again, alongside the theory we will present work from various design studios.

2D DESIGNS

Two-dimensional product design is a representation to scale of a more or less technical drawing of the views of the product to be designed. It is an exact reference that is depicted on a flat two-dimensional surface (paper, computer monitor, etc.) in order to provide the manufacturer with the necessary information for the construction/ production of the design, either in real or conceptual terms.

The garments or objects are often represented with auxiliary views (for details and specifications), clearly indicating their dimensions (measurements); usually a minimum of two projections (views of the object) are required to cover the information relating to the object. Traditionally, technical drawing has used various tools or instruments for 2D design: several kinds of ruler, compasses, pencils, set squares, drawing pens, markers, etc. With computer applications such as CAD, 3D or vector, these tools are no longer required.

Computer tools provide accurate and impressive representations and the designs tend to be viewed better this way (they provide very good information on the garment's dimensions, size and measurements). In the case of textile garment design work, the elevation view is the most important view, one of the main representations of the dihedral system along with the plan view. It is obtained through the parallel projection of the object depicted, where the view is perpendicular to the projection plane, i.e. the clothes are drawn as if they were lying flat on a table. This helps to visualise the piece more clearly. The elevation view, drawn to scale, enables the true dimension of the depicted model to be verified, which is very useful in representations of architectural elements and in textile design, where it forms part of the essential documents for any design project.

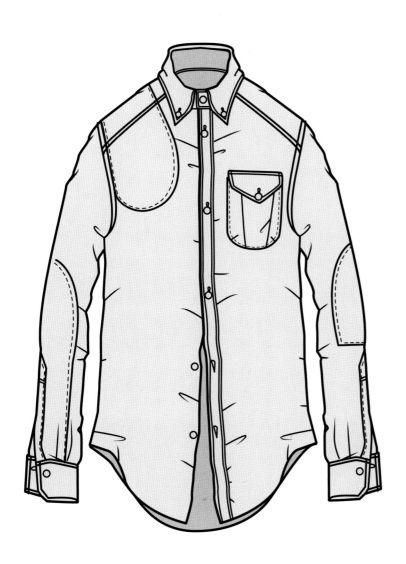

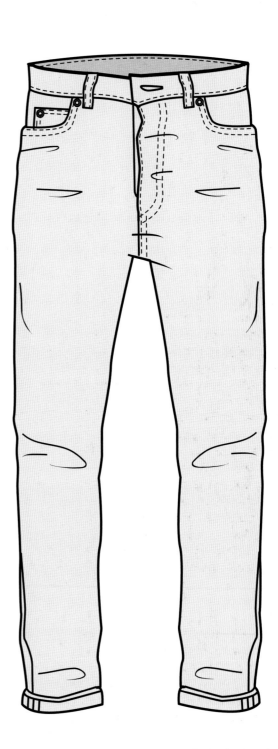

Elevation view representation of a design produced with computer tools. The elevation indicates the volume and details of the model that is represented, which is essential in textile design, where it forms part of the basic description of a garment.

In 2D design, not only must a designer's proposal be original and creative, but also the 2D garment design must be represented with definition and clarity. The 2D design, together with all the additional information required regarding the materials and manufacturing details, comprises the final information available to the manufacturer and the suppliers who produce the product. Some designers usually have some kind of contact with the production companies in order to intervene more easily if there are any doubts or problems during the production process. But it is not always the case. Because of the massive outsourcing of production chains, it is increasingly common not to have any contact with the manufacturer who produces the clothes. If the 2D drawings of a project are not clear and objective, the final producer will not have the necessary information to execute the design, which can cause problems and delays and, at worst, may affect the quality of the final product.

USING VECTOR DRAWING FOR TWO-DIMENSIONAL REPRESENTATIONS

Vector drawing is the essential tool for product design applying the new computer software. We have already discussed the definition of the term 'vector' elsewhere in this book. This is one of the many ways in which a designer can create an image with a rasterised preview of their designs, which can be transferred to other platforms (a printer, plotter or other operating systems).

When you draw a design you can use two types of path, closed paths and open paths. In open paths the first and last nodes are separate. In closed paths the two nodes are joined to close the shape. Depending on where you begin to redraw the path and in what direction you drag, unexpected results could be obtained. For example, a closed path could become an open path, an open path a closed path, or even lose part of a shape by accident. The use of closed shapes (or strokes) enables us to fill the designs with content: either colour, texture, or any bitmap image imported into the final document. When drawing with Bézier curves the famous maxim of 'less is more' applies. The best possible result is obtained with the minimum number of anchor points Someone not used to working with this type of tool might initially tend to use too many anchor points, which will only result in producing more complex drawings that will probably be full of flaws and imperfections. It is essential to simplify paths by removing extra anchor points without changing the shape of the path.

Removing unnecessary anchor points simplifies the artwork, by reducing the file size, and making it display and print faster. It is preferable to draw well-spaced anchor points and practise creating curves by adjusting the length and the angles of the direction lines.

However, most applications that offer technical drawing don't limit you to using vector graphics, as they allow you to import bitmap images from files created in other applications. Most programs recognise all common graphics file formats, making it easy to move art from one application to another, by importing and exporting, or copying and pasting. A key issue relating to 2D designs generated through vector graphics is the practicality of their adjustment for printing – they can be scaled and their definition can be limitlessly increased. For example, you can take the same sectorised design, print it on a business card and afterwards enlarge it and print it on a billboard, maintaining the same level of quality in both images. The most popular document formats for printing are PDF and PostScript.

In the case of a textile garment, the 2D representation should show at least the front and rear elevation views, although a full representation will include details of sleeves, collars, fastenings or folds. If you are designing other products such as footwear or accessories, plan views must be included as well as views of additional details.

A plan view is the representation of the horizontal section of a garment or any other object. It is obtained by a parallel projection, perpendicular to the horizontal plane. There are products which, due to their complexity, require multiple sections and dimensions to be included in their representation. New technologies greatly facilitate this means of representation.

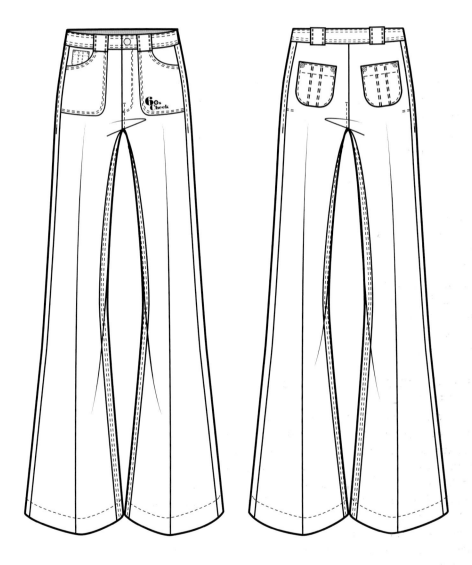

PRINTING WITH A PLOTTER

A plotter is a peripheral printing device that connects to a computer, and is specifically designed for creating vector graphics or line drawings: plans, drawings of parts, etc. Using the plotter, high-quality graphic prints can be obtained that are not possible using a conventional printer. Plotters are aimed primarily at technical drawing and other specialised computer-aided design purposes, especially in cases where it is necessary to work in a high resolution with large format paper.

RASTER

A vector or raster image incorporates a data structure or data file that represents a grid, called the raster, which can be viewed on a computer monitor, paper or other display medium.

Most vector drawing programs enable line representations of the proposed designs. Computer design allows you to add details, seams and finishes easily and accurately. Designs in the women's handbags line for the Autumn / Winter 08-09 collection.

APPLICATIONS FOR 2D DESIGN OF GARMENTS

Computer-Aided Design, better known by its acronym CAD, uses a wide range of computer tools that assist professional designers in various stages of their work. When we start designing a fashion industry product (textiles, leather, shoes, jewellery, etc.), we find a huge range of applications that are extremely sophisticated and specialised for each sector. They offer specific features for each, taking into consideration the characteristics of each type of product, such as materials, specification of measurements, scales, finishes, etc. Typically these applications are aimed at professional and educational use as opposed to home and everyday use of new technologies, as they require a high degree of specialisation and some training in the use of drawing tools. In these pages we will discuss several of the programs available on the market so as to offer readers a choice according to their needs and degree of specialisation.

At the same time, there are other more general design programs, usually offered by large multinational companies, which, although they are less specialised, also allow optimum work development in all cases, depending on the type of product that is to be designed. These programs are not very specialised and do not normally contain sector-specific information, but they are simple to work with and have enormous possibilities. In fact, nowadays most of the design studios consulted for this book frequently use them instead of the more specific applications for several reasons: they are simple to use, easily found, have advanced compatibility, an excellent price and universal features.

2D GARMENT DESIGN WITH ADOBE® ILLUSTRATOR®
There is virtually no design studio without Adobe Illustrator
among its software. It is not a specialised fashion product design
program but its ease of use and enormous benefits have made it
one of the most popular programs in the global panorama of
fashion and textile design. In fact, a whole project can be carried
out (including concept, 2D drawings, figures, fabric design and
printing, etc.) using only this program's tools. Versatility is
probably one of its main features.

If a piece of work has been started outside the Illustrator
environment, you will find that the program is perfectly
compatible with other Adobe products as well as a wide range
of other companies' file formats.

Illustrator supports most Photoshop data, including layer
compositions, layers, editable text and paths. This means that you
can transfer files between Photoshop and Illustrator without
losing the ability to edit the artwork. If the drawing that you are
importing consists of flat colours, these are added to the
Illustrator 'Swatches' panel as custom colours with the same
name as in Photoshop. In this way, the imported colours separate
correctly. Similarly, files in PDF (Portable Document Format) and
EPS (EncapsulatedPostScript) formats can also be incorporated
into your Illustrator design. When you open or embed an EPS file
that was created in another application, Illustrator converts all the
objects to native Illustrator objects. However, if the file contains
data that Illustrator does not recognise, some loss of information
may occur. In addition, EPS format does not support
transparency; therefore it is not a good choice for placing
transparent artwork from other applications into Illustrator. Files
with other formats such as DCS (Desktop Colour Separation), as
well as most AutoCAD data are also compatible with Illustrator,
although as these formats are not very common in the fashion
industry, we shall not consider them in greater depth.

When drawing designs, the new versions of Adobe Illustrator
include an improved operating performance in key operations,

When using vector drawing for our designs,
Adobe Illustrator allows us a faster screen redraw.
To start a front view design, we need to draw the body of
half of our design, then invert a copy of our original
design to attach it to the other half. This way we can
ensure the design is perfectly symmetrical. To finish off
our work, we add all the accessory elements (zippers,
buttons, appliqués).

enabling faster screen redraw when moving, enlarging, scaling
and transforming objects. In addition, you can position objects
and anchor points with expert precision using smart guides and
the align, transform, and control panels. Similarly, you can align
and distribute anchor points with one click using the Control
panel options, or quickly remove areas of artwork with the
Eraser tool and enjoy complete control over the width, shape
and smoothness of the erasure.

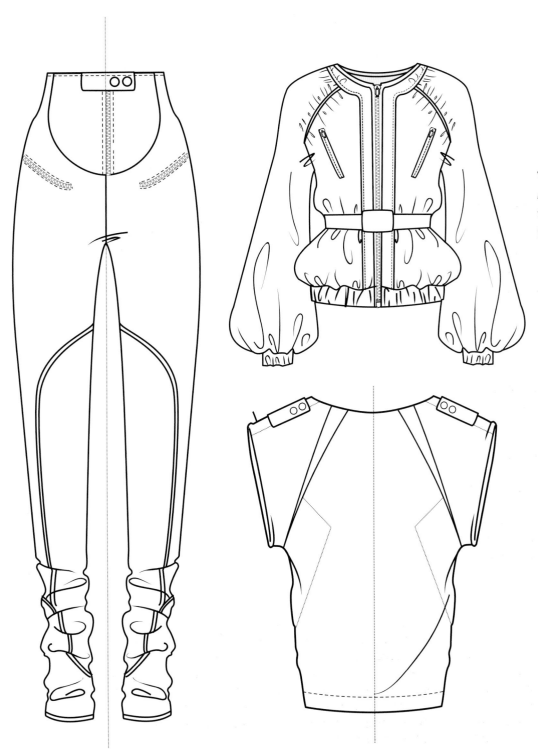

THE MOST IMPORTANT TOOLS

Amongst the most important controls and tools for drawing designs, the following features are worth highlighting:

• LIVE TRACE: with this feature, you can quickly and accurately convert scanned drawings, photographs or other bitmap images into vector paths. If you prefer to manually trace sketches (using the pencil or pen drawing tools), you can use template layers. These non-printed layers are dimmed to 50% so you can easily see any paths you draw in front of the layer.

• PEN: is used for precision drawing and to obtain complete control over the anchor points and Bézier curves.

• PENCIL: lets you draw on the screen in the same way as you would on paper.

• SMOOTHING: is used to quickly smooth unwanted bumps in a path.

• STROKE OPTIONS: you use the stroke panel to control whether a line is solid or dashed. Specifies the stroke weight, the stroke alignment, the style of line joins and line caps and whether the stroke is inside, in the centre or outside the path.

Brushes let you stylise the appearance of vector paths. You can apply brush strokes to existing paths, or you can use the Paintbrush tool to draw a path and apply a brush stroke simultaneously. You can also apply brushstrokes to a line created with any drawing tool, including the 'Pencil' and 'Brush' tools or basic shape tools. In Illustrator, there are four types of brushes – calligraphic, scatter, art and pattern. You can achieve the following effects using these brushes:

- CALLIGRAPHIC BRUSHES. Create strokes that resemble those drawn with the angled point of a calligraphic pen, drawn along the centre of the path.

- SCATTER BRUSHES. Disperse copies of an object (such as a type of seam, finish or decorative element, etc.) along the path.

- ART BRUSHES. Modify the shape of a brush or object evenly along the length of the path.

- PATTERN BRUSHES. Paint a pattern – made of individual modules – that is repeated along the path. Pattern brushes can include up to five tiles, for the sides, inner corner, outer corner, beginning, and end of the pattern. Scatter brushes and pattern brushes can often achieve the same effect. However, one way in which they differ is that pattern brushes follow the path exactly, while scatter brushes do not, therefore all fashion designers normally refer to use scatter brushes.

You can create new calligraphic, scatter, art and pattern brushes based on your own settings; brushes with types of seams (simple, double, small or large stitches, etc.), final garment details, trimmings, etc. For scatter, art, and pattern brushes, you need to create the artwork you want to use beforehand.

CUSTOM BRUSHES

Creating custom brushes can greatly simplify our work, as you can create a brush based on any vector stroke. Any stroke or element that we use regularly can be transformed into a brush and used in all our future work without having to draw it again, as we can store it in our brush library. In this way, we can store brushes with the finishes of different materials, seams or rivets. Like any vector stroke, the colour, weight, etc. of our custom brushes can be subsequently modified using the normal program controls.

To create artwork for brushes:

- The artwork cannot contain gradients, blends, other brush strokes, mesh objects, bitmap images, graphics, placed files, or masks.

- The artwork for art and pattern brushes cannot contain text. To achieve a brush-stroke effect with text, you need to create an outline of the text and then create the brush with this outline.

- For pattern brushes, create up to five pattern tiles (depending on the brush configuration), and add the tiles to the 'Swatches' panel.

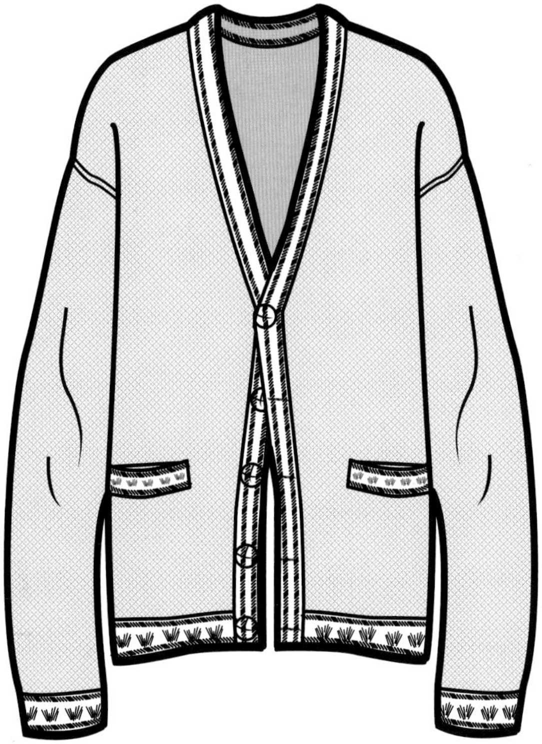

BRUSH LIBRARIES

Brushes are stored in brush libraries. These are collections of preset brushes that form part of Illustrator. You can open multiple brush libraries to browse through their contents and select the brushes that you want to include in the library. You can also add brushes that have been especially created for a project and delete those you don't want to keep. These libraries can be used time and time again, and optimise the use of brushes in each design.

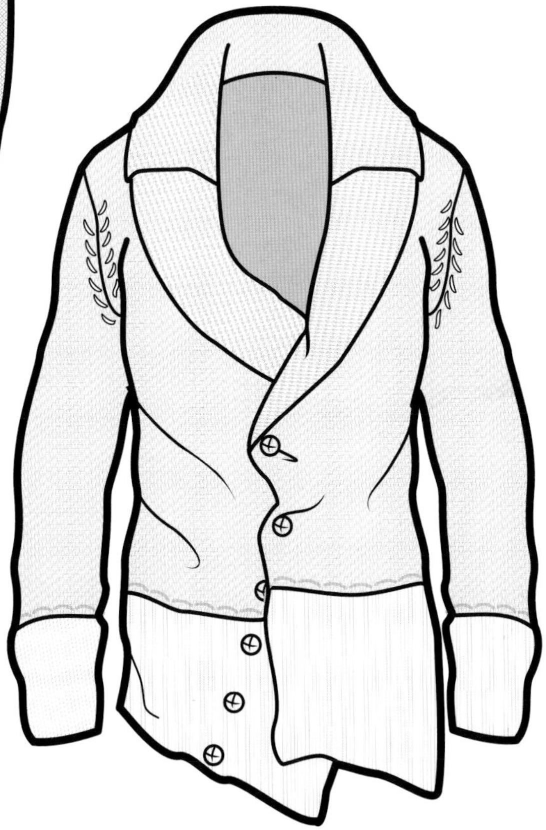

Online clothing designs for the season
Autumn / Winter 08-09.
© WGSN. www.wgsn.com

THE APPEARANCE PANEL

The appearance panel allows you to create multiple fills and strokes for the same object. Adding multiple fills and strokes to an object is the starting point for creating many interesting effects. For example, you can create a second, narrower stroke on top of a wider stroke, or you can apply an effect to one fill but not the other.

There are designs, for example tricot garments, or fabrics with openwork, that need to be filled with a sharp geometric structure. To simulate the effect of these materials the technique most commonly used by professional designers is to apply a pattern.

Online women's clothing designs for the *Charlie Girl* collection, Autumn / Winter 08-09. ©WGSN. www.wgsn.com

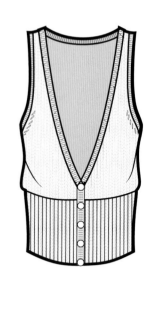

Illustrator offers two methods of painting: the first is to assign a fill, a stroke or both to an entire object. When you have drawn the item with strokes you assign it a fill. This way you can paint other objects, which may be superimposed on the initial drawing.

The result is similar to a collage made up of numerous cuttings from coloured paper. The second converts the object to a live paint group, assigning fills or strokes to the separate edges and faces of paths within it. This method lets you paint as if it were a traditional colour tool. This means you can draw several paths and then colour each area enclosed by these paths (called a face) separately without having to worry about the stacking of objects or layers. You can also change the edge (the path between intersections) by assigning different stroke colours and varying their weight. Using this method, each face and edge can be given a different colour. It has the added advantage that as you move and reshape paths, the edges and faces adjust automatically.

PATTERNS

Some designs need to be filled with a marked geometric structure. For these cases, Illustrator contains a far more powerful tool for working with millimetre precision, which are patterns. Illustrator comes with many patterns that you can access in the 'Swatches' panel and in the 'Illustrator Extras' folder on the Illustrator CD. You can customise existing patterns and design patterns from scratch with any of the Illustrator tools. Patterns intended for filling objects (fill patterns) differ in design and tiling from patterns intended to be applied to a path with the Brushes panel (brush patterns). For best results, use fill patterns to fill objects and brush patterns to outline objects.

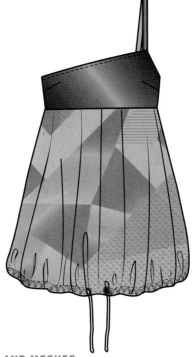

The gradient features allow us to simulate volume and three dimensions in our designs. They are also perfect simulators of metallic or very shiny finishes.

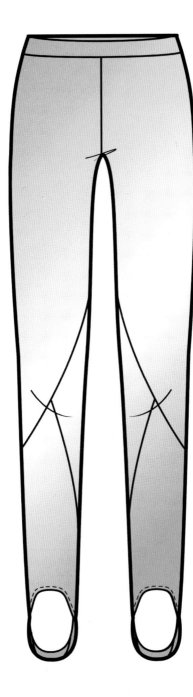

Online women's clothing designs for the
for the Autumn / Winter 08-09 collection.
© WGSN. www.wgsn.com

LIVE PAINT

Live Paint is an intuitive way to create coloured drawings. It lets you use the full range of Illustrator's vector drawing tools, but treats all the paths you draw as though they were on the same flat surface. That is, none of the paths is behind or in front of any other. Instead, the paths divide the drawing surface up into areas, any of which can be coloured, regardless of whether the area is bounded by a single path or by multiple path segments. Once you have created a live paint group, each path remains fully editable. When you move or adjust a path's shape, the colours that had previously been applied do not just stay where they were, like they do in natural media paintings or image editing programs. Instead, Illustrator automatically reapplies them to the new regions that are formed by the edited paths.

GRADIENTS AND MESHES

Depending on the desired effect, we can use the following methods to apply colour gradients to objects:

Gradient fill: a good way to create a smooth colour gradation across one or more objects. You can save the resulting gradients as a swatch to apply to multiple objects.

Mesh object: the best tool if we want to create a single, multicoloured object on which colours can flow in different directions – and transition smoothly from one point to another. By creating a fine mesh on an object and manipulating the colour characteristics at each point in the mesh you can precisely manipulate the colouring of the mesh object.

These features allow us to simulate volume and three dimensions in our designs.

Another tool that has been significantly improved in recent versions of Adobe Illustrator are 'Clipping masks' which are perfect for hiding areas of an object or group, cropping placed images or cutting intricate shapes. This is the perfect tool for adding scanned images of fabrics, vector graphics or patterns to our designs.

A clipping mask (which is the same as a clipping path in Photoshop) is an object whose shape masks other artwork so that only areas that lie within the shape are visible—in effect, clipping the artwork to the shape of the mask. The clipping mask and the objects that are masked are called a clipping set and are marked with a dotted line in the 'Layers' panel.

It consists of a vector path which placed in front of any artwork element (a path or bitmap image) and grouped with the element, hides everything outside the path, without deleting it. Its operation is quite simple: create the clipping path, place it in front of or above the object you want to mask, select both of these and create the clipping mask from the 'Object' menu. To release objects from the effect of a clipping mask, just select the group or the layer that contains the clipping mask and go to 'Object' to 'Release' the mask that has been created. If you want to move the masked object, but not the masking path, simply select the object with the 'Direct Selection' tool (the white arrow). Otherwise, the object and the path will behave as if they were grouped. Objects hidden by clipping masks are still counted in terms of weight and geometry when using an element, which is important to bear in mind in order to avoid very large files.

The paths of clipping masks do not have any colour (fill or stroke). If they originally had colour, they lose it (and do not recover it when the clipping mask is released). Another important feature of clipping masks is that they do not allow partial transparency. They either cover or they show, but they cannot reveal 50% of what is underneath – opacity masks are used for this purpose.

CLIPPING MASKS

The following guidelines apply to the creation of clipping masks:

- The objects that you mask are moved into the clipping mask's group in the 'Layers' panel if they are not already there.

- Only vector objects can be clipping masks; however, any artwork can be masked.

- If you use a layer or group to create a clipping mask, the first object in the layer or group masks everything that is a subset of the layer or group.

- Regardless of its previous attributes, a clipping mask changes to an object with no fill or stroke.

The 'Clipping mask' tool is perfect for adding scanned images of fabric, vector graphics or patterns to our designs, so that we can simulate the final look of the garment with its colour or print effect.
In the same way, we can place any element fitting its shape within the mask of our vector path.

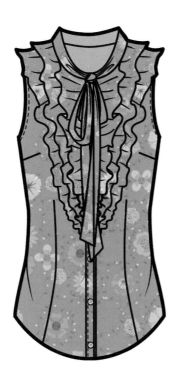

PHOTOSHOP FILTERS

The latest versions of Illustrator incorporate elements of other Adobe programs. Photoshop and Illustrator work so well together you can even use 'Photoshop filters' in Illustrator. However since Illustrator is a vector-based program and Photoshop is bitmap-based, in order to apply the Photoshop filters, you need first to transform an Illustrator drawing to a bitmap graphic. To convert or interpret Illustrator drawings, you need to select 'Rasterise' (from the 'Object' window menu) in the main menu. In the dialogue box that appears, select the target colour model and resolution before accepting. At this point, Illustrator converts the drawing into a bitmap graphic. You can now apply a Photoshop filter to your Illustrator drawing.

Opacity masks are a relatively new Adobe Illustrator feature compared with clipping masks. Their operation is much more flexible and complex. Opacity masks are created similarly to clipping masks: the mask is placed above the object that will be masked. The effect of the opacity mask depends on the original colour of the masking object. The darker it is, the more it covers, and the lighter it is, the more it reveals underneath (intermediate shades of colour or tones hint at what is underneath the mask). This is one of the key differences between opacity and clipping masks: opacity masks allow partial transparency. This is the way to create in Illustrator, for example, a gradient from a colour to transparent.

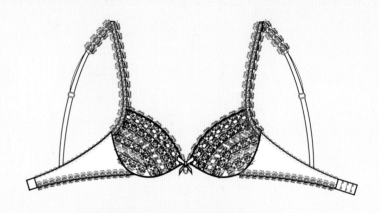

Images of Gisela Intimates' designs for its
Suite Collection line.
© Gisela Intimates.

Yolanda Ferrer, creative director of the label,
discusses the importance in the
lingerie sector of incorporating new
technologies and the new design software
to represent their garments: 'In our
studio, software design tools are universally used.
In Gisela's development we primarily use
Illustrator as the main design software.
Our designs are full of details, we
need the help of custom brushes
– or pattern brushes – that represent our lace,
lace edging or trims, as well as different
seam finishes, zig-zag, double stitch, and so on.
Without these tools our garment design work
would be a lot more complicated.'

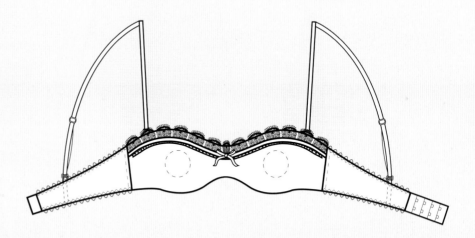

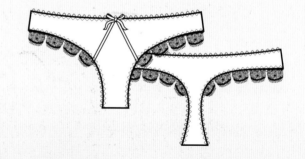

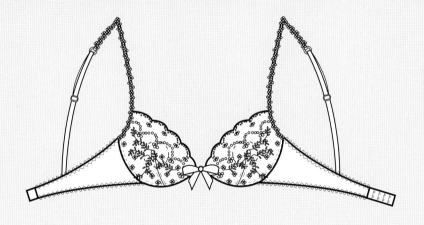

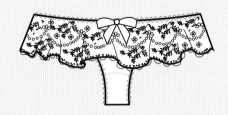

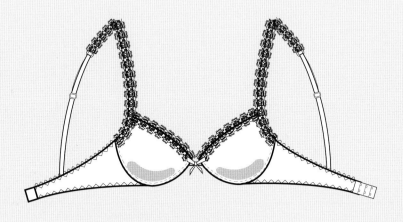

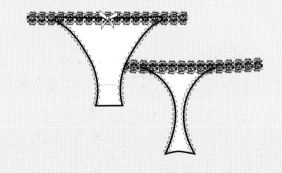

GISELA INTIMATES

Diseño y Fantasía, S.L. is the company behind the Gisela Intimates label, a Málaga-based fashion company that designs, produces and markets women's lingerie. With over three decades of industry experience, highly-skilled staff and constant technological improvement, Gisela is a leading worldwide name in the lingerie industry. Its avant-garde design, exclusive fabrics and above all, highly competitive prices have made Gisela a benchmark for the industry.

www.gisela.com

T-shirt designs from the American creator of the Jeremyville street and sportswear products. www.jeremyville.com

2D GARMENT DESIGN WITH PHOTOSHOP
Although we have already mentioned that the Photoshop application was originally developed for processing raster images (also called bitmaps), the program's possibilities are much greater, including powerful tools for representation and simulation of 2D designs. The drawing tools (the pen and shape tools) let you create and edit vector shapes. In this way you can work with shapes in shape layers or use them as paths. You can also use rasterised shapes, which can be edited with the painting tools.

Photoshop provides multiple pen tools. The 'Standard pen' tool draws with the greatest precision, whereas the ''Freeform pen'' tool draws paths as if you were drawing with pencil on paper. The Magnetic pen option lets you draw paths that snap to the edges of defined areas in your image. You can use the pen tools in conjunction with the shape tools to create complex shapes. Before you begin drawing in Photoshop, you must choose a drawing mode from the options bar. The mode you choose to draw in determines whether you create a vector shape on its own layer, a work path on an existing layer, or a rasterised shape on an existing layer. Vector shapes are lines and curves you draw using the shape or pen tools. They are resolution-independent – they maintain crisp edges when resized, are printed to a PostScript printer, are saved in a PDF file, or imported into a vector-based graphics application. If you prefer, you can create libraries of custom shapes as well as edit a shape's outline (called a path) and attributes (such as stroke, fill colour, and style). Any selection made with a Photoshop selection tool can be defined as a path. Paths are outlines that you can turn into selections, or fill and stroke with colour. The outline of a shape is a path. A path created with Photoshop does not become an image element until you stroke or fill it using a specific colour, a state of the image, a pattern, or a fill layer.

DRAWING WITH THE FREEFORM PEN TOOL
The 'Freeform pen' tool lets you draw as if you were drawing with a pencil on paper. Anchor points are automatically added as you draw. You do not have to determine where the points are positioned as you can adjust them once the path is completed. The 'Magnetic pen' is an option of the 'Freeform pen' tool that lets you draw a path that snaps to the edges of defined areas in a raster image that you want to redraw. The tool lets you define the range and sensitivity of the snapping action, as well as the complexity of the resulting path.

Evolution of a sports shoe design
adding colour and masks with textures and finishes
to the different layers of the work. We started
the process with a line drawing, which was then filled
in with colour effects to represent the end result.

The 'Make work path' command eliminates any feathering applied to the selection. It can also alter the shape of the selection, depending on the complexity of the path and the tolerance value selected. You can easily change the shape of a path by editing its anchor points. Paths can be used in several ways: as a vector mask to hide areas of a layer, as a selection, or simply to fill or outline that path with colour. Another way to draw is by filling pixels. In this way you paint directly on a layer in a similar way to a painting tool. By working in this mode you are creating raster images, not vector graphics. Photoshop offers several features that allow you to use images in other applications. Due to the very close integration between Adobe products, many Adobe applications can directly import Photoshop (PSD) format files and use Photoshop features like layers, layer styles, masks, transparency, and effects. If you only want to use part of a Photoshop image when placing it in another application (for instance, you can use a foreground object and exclude the background), an image clipping path lets you isolate the foreground object and make everything else transparent when the image is printed or placed in another application.

PAINTING AND FILLING DESIGNS WITH COLOUR

Photoshop provides several tools for painting or editing image colour. The 'Brush' and the 'Pencil' tools work like traditional drawing tools, applying colour with brush strokes. The 'Gradient' tool, 'Fill' command and 'Paint bucket' tool apply colour to large areas. Tools like the 'Eraser', 'Blur' or 'Smudge' tools modify the existing colours in the image. Brush tip options control how colour is applied. You can apply colour gradually, with soft edges, with large brush strokes, with various brush dynamics with different blending properties, and with brushes of various sizes. You can also simulate spray paint with an airbrush.

TEXTILSTUDIO, A SPECIALISED APPLICATION FOR
INTEGRAL DESIGN

TextilStudio is a professional design and production software
aimed at textile companies, designers, printers and
manufacturers, technology centres, colleges and the footwear
industry, among many others. It is the most important program
created to date in Spain, and has its own technology and
terminology. TextilStudio has over 150 customers of all levels,
from freelance professionals to companies as emblematic as
Armand Basi, Inditex and Mango. The current version marketed
is TextilStudio 8, which contains significant innovations and
improvements to adapt the program to the industry's new
requirements. It should be noted that the application is fairly
comprehensive and has specialised tools both for the vector
drawing of garments and for the design and processing of prints
or graphics, for preparing professional production data sheets,
with easy access to libraries of symbols, details or base
topology for the preparation of highly specialised product data
sheets. The application is compatible with Mac and Windows
environments, making the software truly universal.

It includes a complete set of specialised tools for the fashion
industry. As it is a design program, it contains powerful vector
drawing tools which let you create designs from scratch or from
a scanned drawing and later redraw them vectorally. Its libraries
contain extremely useful tools such as stitch libraries (with types
of seams, finishes, stitch length, etc.), button collections, zippers,
pins, etc. Naturally, these basic libraries can be completed by
customising their content in line with our interests. These
elements can be easily coloured and also modified to finish off
the work.

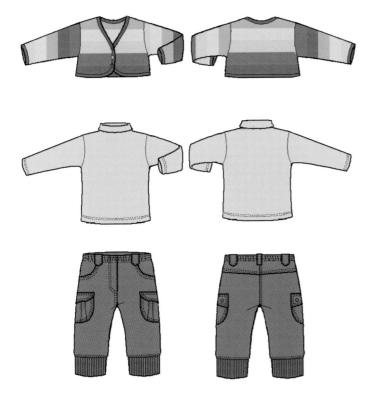

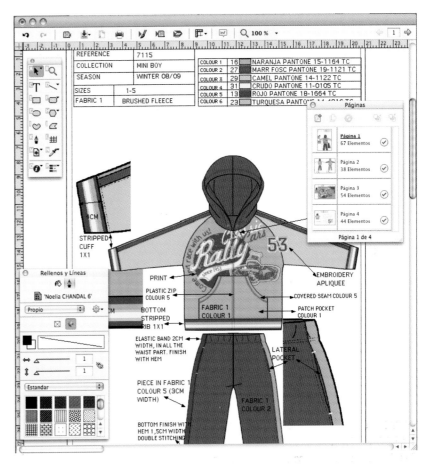

Commercial designs created using the tools provided by the TextilStudio program, based on vector drawing, customising designs with its full collections of textures, finishes and textile editors to represent any material that you are going to use.

When it comes to colouring the design, TextilStudio includes a comprehensive and easy-to-use colour gradient editor and colour libraries, as well as complete collections of textures, finishes and textile editors, finishes and textile editors to simulate any material that you are going to used. In this way, you can depict gingham wool or houndstooth just by dragging the fill to your drawing, greatly saving on work time. TextilStudio lets you colour your designs by accessing its colour libraries. To colour you simply drag the colours to the areas that interest you. The libraries can be created manually or imported from other programs, including Pantone swatch libraries. It also includes tools for creating colour variations of designs easily and conveniently. In addition, TextilStudio contains powerful tools for managing prints – it can reduce the colour, adapt it to your libraries and quickly and flexibly create compositions.

The best thing is that we do not have to redraw the pattern, as these features can be applied directly from a scanned image (and the colour and shape can be refined with its specific features). Undoubtedly, the most outstanding characteristic of TextilStudio is its easy, user-friendly interface and assimilation. The program features 'catalogues' – this area allows you to locate all the information you need with just one click and is a great help for working quickly and easily. TextilStudio is also fully compatible with most usual formats, both vector images and bitmaps. You can open any file edited outside TextilStudio without any problems simply by dragging it to your work area and including it your design.

The TextilStudio interface enables us to organise all this product-related information in 'catalogues', which are windows that preview all the files stored in that category. We can view them all simultaneously, print them, rapidly access the desired item, copy an image or duplicate it without having to open it, etc. These catalogues can store elements like colouring, embroidery, prints, details of garments or trimmings, and history of shapes and bases of the collection. This means that the application includes a library of fragments of garment designs and garment details, which you can use as a starting point. In addition, the TextilStudio catalogue can store images to be fully or partly reused at a later date, so that all the information is available at any time to be used, adapted or modified. TextilStudio also lets you create complete technical data sheets including fields with text linked to its own database, information regarding the colours featured in images, textile symbols, and a rich variety of tools (rectangles, ovals, etc.) that enable each company to create its own completely customised profile. If we store our data sheets in the TextilStudio 'catalogue', we can quickly access all previous data sheets, and reuse the layout or part of the content. A key feature is that TextilStudio lets you create multipage datasheets, so you can include all the necessary information to fully define your design. As a final point, we must mention that the corporate website for this design program includes tutorials, demonstration videos and demo downloads, so that any interested reader can go through the information on the program's possibilities before taking a decision on whether to purchase. TextilStudio also offers maintenance courses with an hourly rate for staff working with the program or new team members. The TextilStudio manual can also be consulted, which is a complete video-based course that shows you all the program's options step by step. Another TextilStudio user service is its Job Bank, which links job seekers to job vacancies, both for TextilStudio and the textile industry in general.

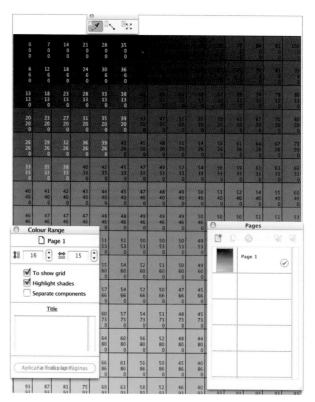

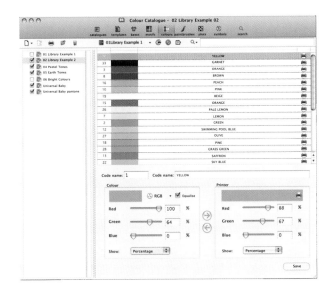

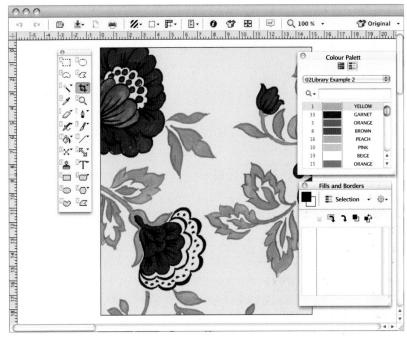

TextilStudio can match your printer and screen colours. It includes a Colour Range Editor, which is essentially for designers to create multiple colour tables on screen to print on their printer. It works very quickly, and using the various program tools an optimum result is achieved in just a few steps. You can also produce a series of gradients between ranges. You just have to create the first and the last page, and TextilStudio adds the intermediate ranges creating a great colour spectrum. The ranges can be edited and customised as the presentation require. The number of columns and lines of colours can be varied for each page as required. The spectrum of colours is finally stored in the Colour Libraries that are subsequently used to colour the designs. The colours in the libraries can even be matched to your printer colours. You have the option of storing and saving libraries by season. TextilStudio can also import libraries from other programs such as Adobe Illustrator.

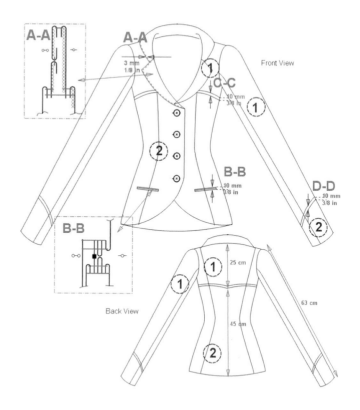

KALEDO, THE PROFESSIONAL DESIGN PLATFORM
CREATED BY LECTRA

Kaledo is the new design software offered by Lectra
(www.lectra.com) for new generations of designers, which will
soon replace U4ia and Prima (other Lectra computer fashion
design programs), as it incorporates the best tools from these
applications. This application has been specifically created for
the creative design and textile area, where designers can create
their own collections. Kaledo is one of the highly specialised
programs aimed at the fashion industry. It provides a virtual,
visual environment for creating and managing fashion
collections. Kaledo removes the technical barriers to creativity,
providing a virtual design environment with powerful,
professional tools which preserve design integrity throughout
the product lifecycle, and allow rapid storyboarding, variations
and updates. Lectra's product covers all requirements from
concept through to consumer, greatly facilitating the product
lifecycle, and has extensive technical expertise.
It lets you define trends and colour combinations for each
season or product line, design garments, choose fabrics and
associated patterns, organise these products into lines to share
with the marketing and sales department, and communicate to
the studio which products have been selected, all activities that
form part of the day-to-day activity of fashion professionals.

As the apparel world evolves, designers need to develop a
greater number of collections per year, create more and more
products per collection and make increasingly personalised
models. By removing many manual processes (such as re-
drawing designs by hand), providing immediate access to digital
libraries, existing fabrics and fibre references, we can simplify
the creation of designs and deliver product variations based on
ideas that have already been successful.

With Kaledo, designers enjoy an unprecedented streamlining
of workflow through the automation or simplification of many
tasks that until now were slow and complicated processes.
Automatic design management instantly reflects changes across
all workflow processes, so that information is continually
updated, reducing the need for meetings and simplifying
prototyping and decision-making.

Through amazingly realistic simulations of prints, weaves and
knits, companies can test designs and production techniques in
the first phases of the specific product's lifecycle. Automatic
colourway management and the ability to instantly incorporate
feedback for onscreen approvals saves time and represents a
further step towards full interactivity.

Kaledo fits designers' needs perfectly: symmetrical drawing,
stitch lines, curves, etc. and enables new styles to be designed
with a single click. You can select from the various available line
styles and thicknesses and use the drawing and filling features,
or text. Kaledo easily defines areas to fill with colour or fabric for
vectorial sketches (or scanned drawings), and the fabric scale,
orientation and positioning for each model. In addition, Kaledo
features a library of standard styles and 'component parts'
(collars, pockets, sleeves, etc.) that can be modified at will and
facilitate the composition of new styles. With Kaledo you can
create storyboards, which are product boards organised by
theme or product line. This facilitates the presentation of
collections to the group of decision makers involved in the
selection of products.

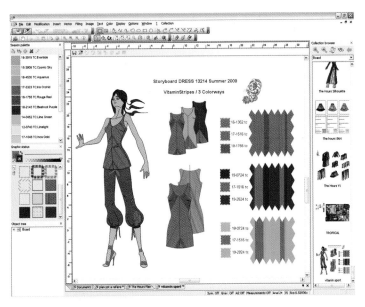

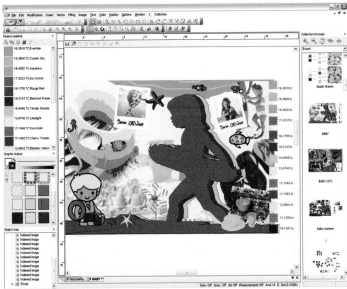

Images provided by Lectra www.lectra.com
showing how the Kaledo program works.

The program provides a functional environment for
the generation and management of fashion creation,
allowing rapid storyboarding, variations and updates.
It enables the definition of trends and colour
combinations for each season or product line,
garment design, choice of fabrics and patterns that we
intend to use.

COLOUR MANAGEMENT

To improve the management of the colour
palette, the colour profile creation tools
enable you to rapidly adapt screen to printed
colours to suit the specific requirements of
your design environment or point of sale.
Working with a calibrated colour palette
allows you to communicate perfectly with your
fabric suppliers or your dyers. The samples
can be evaluated directly on screen or on
paper which greatly accelerates the final
approval process and the colour matching.
The use of colour profiles adapted to graphic
(ICC) or textile (Datacolor) software ensures
you can design and print colours with the best
possible reproduction quality.

In order to obtain these colour verification
profiles, your system also needs to include
the Datacolour CP2000 colorimeter to create
graphic (ICC) or textile (Datacolour) colour
profiles for your screens, or the Spyder
Datacolor colorimetre for creating graphic
(ICC) colour profiles for screens. You can also
complete the system with the Mercury
Datacolour spectrophotometer, for creating
spectral colour palettes (a rainbow) from
colour standards for optimum colour
communication.

The principal advantage of the Kaledo Collection is that it covers all the phases of creation of textile design. Moreover it enables you to:

- Develop different collections very rapidly.

- Structure collections and share data with development teams in real time.

- Improve the decision-making process, by giving designers the ability to illustrate their product data sheets for each of their styles and fully concentrate on design.

- React quickly to the tiniest modifications.

- Save time and reduce the risk of errors.

- Ensure clear communication with teams in charge of developing product specifications.

Both Kaledo Collection and Kaledo Style (Kaledo Collection includes all Kaledo Style's professional design tools, plus some new-generation features) are specialised design platforms for preparing fashion collections, working interactively in a collaborative environment and communicating in real-time with team members. Streamlining workflow not only improves productivity, but also improves profitability. It reduces the number of physical samples (prototypes) required as well as the cost of shipping or courier services.

Kaledo's tools incorporate accurate specifications and production-ready output, simplifying communication with manufacturers and minimising errors and associated rework. It also lets companies streamline the process for launching new collections or product lines according to the latest trends and the expectations and feedback from consumers at point of sale.

In the competitive fashion industry, Lectra's Kaledo Collection solution meets the needs of fashion design departments and enables designers to rapidly create models and test colour and fabric combinations. Communication along the network of the collection plan is simpler and faster, and realistic simulations allow those involved in decision-taking to evaluate the creative concepts more easily, simplifying the decision-making process. Moreover, the technical data relating to the fabric is correctly built-in from the beginning, providing the transfer of reliable data to the clothing manufacturers.

ADD-ON APPLICATIONS: KALEDO KNIT, KALEDO WEAVE AND KALEDO PRINT
The Kaledo program, developed by Lectra, includes three specific applications to respond to the need for creating innovative new fabrics, which attract attention and differentiate products in the fashion industry. While these are applications for creating knits, prints and woven fabrics as opposed to tools for garment design (2D or 3D), we have decided to discuss them together with the other products from the Kaledo range, to facilitate understanding of Lectra's specific application.

The cost of preparing textile samples, the difficulty of ensuring colour consistency, and the added complexity of the rapid presentation of fabric and print designs mean that textile design has become a real challenge for many companies in the industry. The main priority of most companies is to ensure rapid fabric samples that allow validation, as well as effective communication between designers and manufacturers. This has led the Lectra company to launch specific applications for the design of fabrics and prints.

Images of the interface of the add-on application
Kaledo Weave, provided by Lectra.
www.lectra.com

The Kaledo Weave application enables design concepts for
woven designs and textures and their colourways to be
created both extremely easily and with an accurate
simulation, so that communication with the manufacturer
becomes quicker and more efficient.

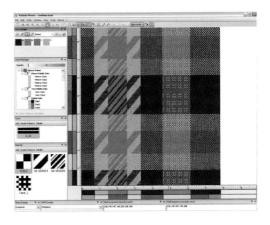

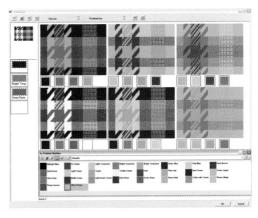

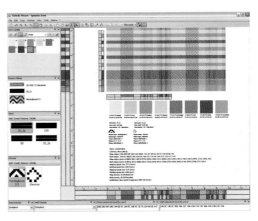

KALEDO AND THE LECTRA SYSTEM

The communication between the Kaledo
application and the Lectra Fashion PLM
system (which we will discuss later) enables
the designers to be worked with directly, since
they have access to all the relevant
information relating to a product or product
lines, which avoids data re-entry and the
resulting time loss and possibility of errors.
The program also includes the applications
Kaledo Print, Kaledo Knit and Kaledo Weave
for printing designs and collections, and for
creating printed, knitted and woven designs. A
final point worth making in this section
regarding the Kaledo family applications is
that there is only a Windows version. The
minimum system requirement for installation
is Windows XP (SP2) Pentium IV 2.8 Ghz, and
a 4 GB RAM server and 450 GB hard drive.

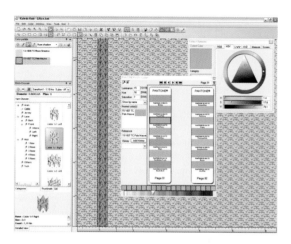

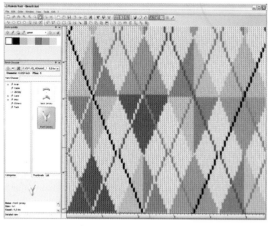

Kaledo Knit enables designers to create, validate and communicate design concepts for professional knits within a user-friendly working environment and a customisable interface (according to the characteristics of the company or designer). Kaledo Knit contains toolbars dedicated to drawing and editing, both for jacquard and structured knits. For designs that include jacquard patterns, the application provides an automatic knit rendering of any bitmap image, and geometric drawing tools and shapes simplifying the composition of new designs. It also gives the choice of front or back jersey representations. To accelerate validation times, its colour combination functions have been simplified for direct comparison on screen, replacing the colour or simply dragging and dropping it (the program includes online colour libraries, such as Pantone, in addition to allowing customisation of the ranges creating your own colour palettes).

For structured knits, Kaledo Knit contains an extensive online library of knit stitches, including jersey, arans, cables and laces. The program itself corrects linking errors between stitches and allows you to customise yarn size and strands, and to add additional layers to simulate embroideries or accessories. For communicating the designs to the rest of the company or manufacturers, Kaledo Knit automatically provides information with various options for automatic layout of the knit panel, its colourways, information about the palette data, stitches, and yarns, with various presentation options available, etc. It also offers the possibility of easy validating of designs via realistic simulation of knit designs due to the use of a 3D virtual knitting machine. Kaledo Knit can be linked to other Kaledo applications.

Images of the interface of the add-on application Kaledo Print, produced by Lectra.
www.lectra.com

Kaledo Print contains Studios dedicated to colour reduction, painting, image cleaning, repeat creation and colourway generation, greatly simplifying the work process for the fashion designer.

RENDERING APPLIED TO FASHION

Rendering is the process of generating an image from a model. Rendering can be done with materials ranging from pencil, pen, felt-tip or pastel, to 2D and 3D digital media. In the rendering process, the computer 'interprets' the scene in three dimensions.

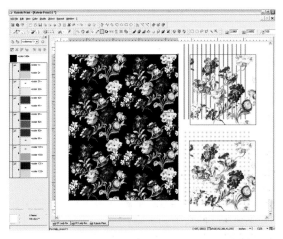

KaledoWeave is the specific tool for creating plain, rib, basket, twill and satin weaves. It offers the possibility of automatically developing patterns and fabric combinations with several yarn types and thickness and different weave patterns in the same woven design. KaledoWeave allows the visual drawing of warp and weft, the tracing of scanned fabrics, and the comparison of as many colourways as you wish. It also features an online library, like the rest of the Kaledo family of applications. Additionally, KaledoWeave provides automated reporting with various options for automatic layout of the weave, its colourways, palette data information, weave patterns, and yarns, as well as the number of shafts needed, all this due to various presentation options available, for validation before final approval. In this way, KaledoWeave considerably reduces the work of verification and subsequent modifications to samples to obtain final approval.

Kaledo Print is an equally intuitive working environment. It contains studios dedicated to colour reduction, drawing (achieving unlimited effects, with customisable brushes), image cleaning, repeat creation, and colourway generation, streamlining the creative process for the textile designer. With it you can obtain feasible printing of work and can control at all times the number of colours needed to produce a design, thus removing the technical barriers to creativity. Like the other textile design applications (Knit and Weave), we obtain a consistent print colour, and with maximum conformity to the original designer's selection, with the Kaledo Colour Match facility.

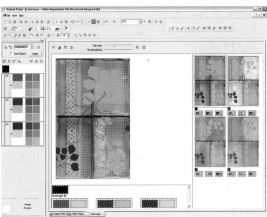

Images of the interface of the add-on application Kaledo Print, produced by Lectra.
www.lectra.com

Kaledo Print contains Studios dedicated to colour reduction, painting, image cleaning, repeat creation and colourway generation, greatly simplifying the work process for the fashion designer.

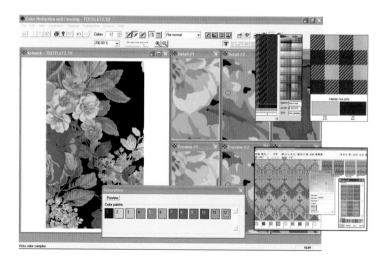

Image of the interface of the Vision Fashion Studio application, www.gerbertechnology.com

Vision Fashion Studio reflects the general trend of programs launched by the different companies for the fashion market, and includes online design features, the development of patterns and fabrics, as well as presentations and data sheets.

VISION® FASHION STUDIO, THE DESIGN STUDIO CREATED BY GERBER TECHNOLOGY

The company Gerber Technology (www.gerbertechnology.com) which produces services for many industries, offers the application Vision Fashion Studio as part of their global services for the fashion sector. Like the other specialised programs we have seen in this chapter, Vision Fashion Studio is a textile design tool with special features for 2D line (vector) representation, together with a broad colour palette and the possibility of developing an overview of the product, including features for design of prints, knitted or flat woven fabrics. It can also be used to create spectacular presentations or product catalogues to accurately display your ideas. Vision Fashion Studio design tools are exclusively offered for Windows, and require a Pentium IV processor (or more recent) and 512MB RAM to run the program.

The programs launched by the various companies for the fashion market tend to be complete packages that include features for online design, development of prints and fabrics, as well as presentations and data sheets. Vision Fashion Studio helps designers create a structured product development in a matter of hours (instead of days or weeks), facilitates the design of custom fabrics and the immediate viewing of results. Designers can even start by scanning prints into the system, reproducing them and reworking them to their taste; it helps designers reduce the large range of colours in scanned images to a defined number of chosen colours. The application cleans misplaced pixels of colour and allows colour separation to be viewed.

With this program it is even possible to preview the image as you work, maintaining the flow of the repeat pattern at all times. The application can provide additional technical information for the fabric manufacturer or the production manager through the automatic creation of technical reports.

In parallel, the application has the ability to create unlimited colour versions of the same design using Pantone textile codes, HSV and RGB values or a customised colour palette. The tools are designed to imitate tasks usually performed by hand. To design knits and weaves in greater depth, the application also provides additional tools for knit design which adds to the features of Vision Fashion Studio. It designs intricate knit patterns by simply drawing with any of the many knit stitches available in the stitch library or can create coordinated knits by capturing motifs from prints, with tools to change stitch styles with a click of the mouse. You can then present your knit design in one of

Designs created with the Vision Fashion Studio application. The application can add additional technical information to our designs, simplifying the task of preparing data sheets for the manufacturer.

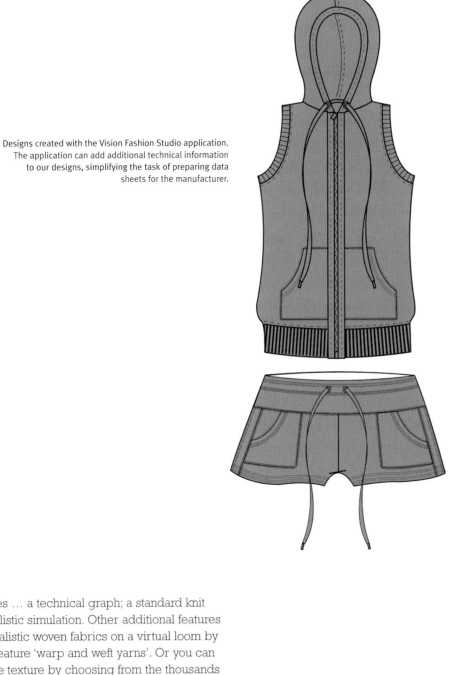

several possible modes … a technical graph; a standard knit symbol chart, or a realistic simulation. Other additional features allow you to design realistic woven fabrics on a virtual loom by merely selecting the feature 'warp and weft yarns'. Or you can create a custom weave texture by choosing from the thousands of available weave patterns. The simulation of shadows will bring your design to life, and there is also the option of the 'Draping' application, whose main function is to quickly and easily drape fabrics on sketches or photographs to simulate three-dimensional draping, obtaining reliable and valid representations that simplify the creative process.

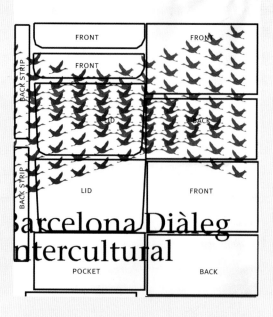

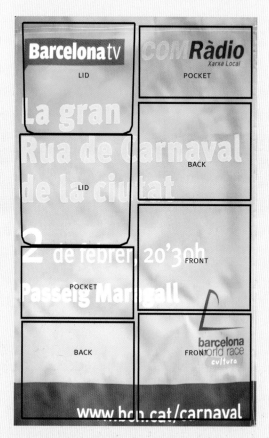

SELECTING THE BEST PROGRAM

We can see from our discussion that there is a wide-ranging and comprehensive range of applications. There are very specific tools, with detailed and simplified features, but, however many features a program has, it can never replace the creative and human process of any job. There is no miraculous software that automatically develops, without human involvement, all the stages from conceptualisation of a product to its final representation. Therefore, the best program will always be the one in which we can individually best express our emotions, concerns and creative expectations. As a result, you can find design studios that use some of the programs we have described (which are probably the leading applications in the sector) but, at the same time, there are other professionals who use less computer tools or opt for more general applications such as CorelDraw or Photoshop. There are also designers who still use Freehand as their main vector tool (the situation of the program in recent years has already been discussed earlier in this book). The possibilities are so broad that we prefer readers to take their own decisions based on their own experience, environment or capabilities. However, we recommend all designers to continually refresh their training and to analyse in detail the various options available on the market. A careful choice of systems can have a great impact in substantial savings both on work time and the cost of manufacturing or production of prototypes.

Designs from Demano. Barcelona 2008.

'When we graduated as architects, we worked in the design of exhibitions and furniture. We worked for museums and cultural institutions. This helped us when we presented our project idea to the Barcelona City Council. Since we trained as architects, the best program we knew from our degree was Autocad. Amazing, we still use it for the design of the bags.'

DEMANO

Demano arose with the idea of reusing PVC and turning it into bags and objects for daily use. The brand was created in Barcelona in 1999. The founders are Colombian and have been living in Barcelona since 1998. Demano consists of three associates, Liliana Andrade, Marcela Manrique and Eleonora Parachini. From time they arrived in Barcelona the volume of communication material produced in the city year-round attracted their attention. They were particularly interested in the hanging banners on all the street poles in the city, which were promoting exhibitions, events and cultural festivals. One day they met workers dismantling some of the banners and, realising the qualities of the material (tough, flexible, waterproof, reusable), they asked for some. With these initial banners they made bags for themselves but, after showing them to several people, they realised the potential of the material and how interesting it would be to develop a project. At this point the idea of submitting a proposal to Barcelona City Council emerged, with the aim of giving a second life to all this material, produced every year and thrown away without any kind of ecological awareness. They started researching everything about the material and its development process, and sat down to prepare the project to submit to the City Council. That is when the Demano project and brand were created. They reached agreements with Barcelona City Council and with all the cultural bodies who produce the banners, ICUB, Fundació Tàpies, the MACBA (*Museu d'Art Contemporani de Barcelona*), CCCB (*Centre de Cultura Contemporània de Barcelona*) for the management of the waste materials used in promoting their corporate events.

Line drawing applied to pattern and marker design

Once the design phase has been completed, the production phase begins, which uses different materials and specific production techniques for each. The market reality compels us to diversify production by contracting outside companies to take responsibility for these tasks. It is worth remembering that very few companies still have full structures in place for design, pattern-making and production.

Fashion as an industry has undergone a giant revolution. The challenges that companies are facing on a day-to-day basis include reducing product development times, ensuring a perfect fit and grading in all their garments, improving communication and taking advantage of pattern design applications that are simpler and easier to use. Vector line drawing, as explained at the beginning of the chapter, is not only used in the fashion industry for representing designs, but also has an operational function and enables some of the most complex production and manufacturing processes to be automated, especially tasks such as grading of patterns and marker-making to make better use of the area or cut of the fabric. The wide-ranging supply in the industry has evolved over time, following the merger of various technological groups. There are currently three main groups providing professional services specifically for the fashion production sector, which are: Lectra (which historically acquired the technological company Investronica), Gerber and Optitex. Each group offers an extensive and specialised range, all three companies are distributed in Spain and their applications are usually included in the curricula of professional fashion and garment manufacturing courses. Naturally, there are other options on the market, but they are less commonly used, less standardised and their distribution and services are more limited. Throughout this section we will try to guide the reader by highlighting the most innovative proposals available on the market although, as always, we advise you to complete this information by downloading demonstrations and videos to help visualise the possibilities inherent in each product.

Vector drawing represents a breakthrough for the professional fashion industry: it facilitates the automation of more complex processes that require a higher dedication of resources and time.

CAM (COMPUTER-AIDED MANUFACTURING)

Computer-aided manufacturing involves of the use of computers and new technologies to assist in all phases of product development, including the planning of the process and production, mechanisation, timing, administration and quality control. The CAM system covers many of these technologies. Given its advantages, computer-aided design and manufacturing tend to be combined in CAD/CAM systems. This combination allows the transfer of information from the design stage to the planning stage for the manufacturing of a product, without the need to manually recapture the garment's geometric data. The database which is developed in CAD is stored, then processed by the CAM to obtain the necessary data and instructions to operate and thereby monitor the production machinery, the material management team and the automated testing and inspection to establish the product quality.

LECTRA'S COMPUTER PATTERN DESIGN SOLUTIONS: MODARIS AND PGS

Designed to meet the demands of customers all over the world and their specific needs in terms of quality and fit of garments, Modaris has probably been the most widely-used application in the fashion market for over 10 years. The new version offers added value. Combining design and production, Lectra's pattern making and grading solution enables patterns to be rapidly produced for all types of fabrics, from the simplest to the most complex, such as lingerie or *haute couture*. Depending on the situation, Modaris can increase production by as much as 50%. Its great ability to exchange information with other CAD systems on the market makes it an essential application for companies working on the network (with multiple sites, partners and subcontractors in various countries).

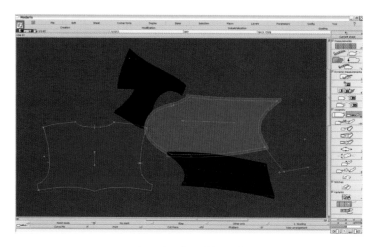

Image interface of the Modaris program, created by Lectra.
www.lectra.com

THE THREE FORMATS OF MODARIS

The new version of the program is available in three formats, which adapt to companies' profiles and the level of expertise of their work teams in modelling and grading, as well as their productivity requirements:

- Modaris-Mode: the core of the pattern-making solutions, it simplifies product development, particularly if it is integrated with Easy Grading, Lectra's new automated grading application.

- Modaris-ModePro: advanced functions which optimise pattern creation, also with Easy Grading.

- Modaris-ExpertPro: the pattern design solution that improves design departments' productivity, due to the exclusive concept of all-size pattern design.

THE PGS SYSTEM

With PGS, Lectra offers a new version of its modelling solution. With a fully task-orientated interface, the PGS system allows you to create patterns quickly and share them with colleagues, using its interoperability features. With the new version, you can optimise the creation and adjustment of patterns through features such as automating repeat designs, transformation and industrialisation, and of course, grading (it also uses the Easy

Grading technology). Fully integrated into the cycle of product development, PGS can be perfectly adapted to the user's level of experience owing to its three versions, which enable you to develop your modelling teams' creativity:

- PGS Formula: the simplest version of the software program for creating patterns and subsequent grading.

- PGS Indus: the solution that simplifies the tasks of creation, verification, modification, industrialisation and grading.

- PGS Model: an advanced automated solution for creating simple or complex patterns and their subsequent industrialisation.

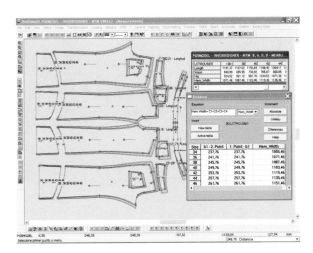

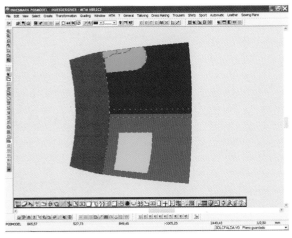

Image interface of the Modaris program, created by Lectra.
www.lectra.com

With the new versions of the industrial pattern-making
systems created by Lectra, we can use the latest scaling
functions, in particular the Easy Grading tool.

NEW SCALING FUNCTION

All the applications use a new grading function developed by
Lectra to adapt to the new requirements. Whether carried out
internally or outsourced (within the same country or thousands
of miles away), grading remains an essential step in collection
development. The grading phase ensures that a garment can be
produced in any size and guarantees the end quality. Once the
basic pattern has been produced and the technical
specifications defined the garment needs to be reproduced in
different sizes. To do this, professionals must be perfectly familiar
with the rules of grading (which can make outsourcing more
difficult) and use measurement tables which are more or less
accurate or representative of the population's physical
measurements as well as the ad hoc functions of the modelling
software.

In a context where the number of collections is continually
increasing, fashion industry professionals are interested in
optimising this phase of product development in terms of time
and cost, by making the grading process easier and faster,
satisfying quality requirements while at the same time ensuring
the perfect fit of garments. There is therefore a need to
implement an intuitive, efficient and fully-automated scaling
solution.

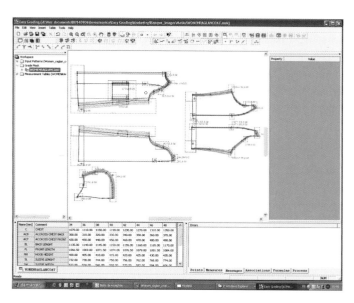

Image of the Easy Grading system created by Lectra.
www.lectra.com

With the new automated grading application,
the process of optimisation of patterns and sizes
is convenient and fast.

The new feature, which makes the grading process within the Lectra programs easier and faster, is called Easy Grading. The application satisfies quality requirements while contributing to perfectly-fitting garments. Easy Grading, included in the latest versions of Lectra's pattern design solutions (Modaris and PGS), is an intelligent automated grading application. With the new automated grading application, the user selects a graphic representation (or a 'mask' or template) with grading information by product type (trousers, shirts, skirts, etc.) from a customised library. After selecting a measurement chart, the operator loads the pattern pieces and positions them onto the mask either manually or automatically. The grading is then performed with a simple click of the mouse. Easy Grading's ability to deal with different measurement tables enables clothing-sector companies to customise the grading of each garment according to the specific needs of local populations. This innovation, the result of over 30 years experience in the clothing industry, is based on Lectra's patented calculation method; it allows the majority of patterns (trousers, shirts, skirts, etc.) to be graded in just a few clicks and the sharing of valuable grading knowledge throughout the company, with the added advantage that the teams can improve their grading expertise, capitalising on the best practices.

MODARIS 3D FIT AND LECTRA FASHION PLM

Both PGS and Modaris can now be combined with Modaris 3D Fit, Lectra's new 3D virtual prototyping solution, to ensure the fit of all garments and to validate their style. The applications can both be integrated with Lectra Fashion PLM, for the management of the collection life cycle that accelerates and rationalises the collection development process.

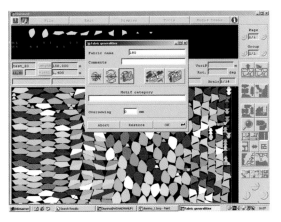 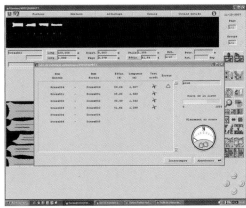 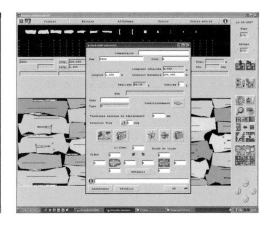

Images of the DiaminoFashion interface, marker-making software designed by Lectra. www.lectra.com.

DiaminoFashion is designed for operating plain or printed fabrics. Its functions are included in pattern design programs to improve their performance. It also offers options to optimise marker-making in all kinds of materials, with considerable saving in materials.

DIAMINOFASHION AND MGS, PLUG-INS FOR LECTRA PATTERN DESIGN PROGRAMS

Both applications are ideal additions for pattern design since they increase marker-making productivity, i.e. the distribution of the pieces on the fabric surface, optimising the cut, respecting the fabric threads, pattern or texture. This interactive and automatic marker-making application offers an effective and proven response to a clearly identified need for an application with the same degree of fabric optimisation as an experienced user. DiaminoFashion is seamlessly integrated with the Modaris pattern-making program in the same way that MGS complements the functions of the PGS application for pattern design. Both applications can reduce nesting time so that a greater number of combinations can be tested, in addition to costing operations and production, with results comparable or superior to those obtained through expert manual processing.

All the functions of both the programs are designed to improve performance, which can mean a significant saving in material, as well as allowing new markers to be generated from existing ones by analogy or addition of articles. Both MGS and DiaminoFashion are available in different modules and with different options to suit user experience and needs. The MGS Server option is of particular interest, which allows you to perform marker-making with a server. This configuration automatically shares markers between workstations as well as automatic marker-making. With this application, different production sites can work online without losing work control of and with quick and easy access to the full information to do a specific follow-up.

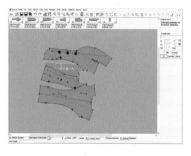
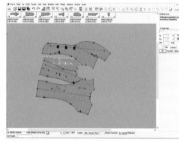
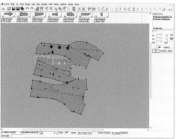
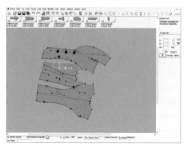

ACCUMARK, GERBER TECHNOLOGY'S PATTERN DESIGN PROGRAM

Gerber's AccuMark software is specifically designed for the fashion industry, for pattern-making, grading and marker-making. It brings enormous benefits for pattern design and other uses to satisfy the need for rapid changes required by the fashion industry. Accumark allows you to automate tasks to achieve greater agility in collections and production. By electronically storing data, it gives the security that these will not be lost (it is protected from natural disasters) and saves space for day-to-day work.

The 'Pattern Wizard' included in the AccuMark application provides predefined and pregraded garment types for men, women and children, with the aim of speeding up pattern design. You can create new patterns or modify existing ones for new styles, performing several operations simultaneously or using the advanced dart, fullness, draping and pleat capabilities. In parallel, patterns for costings can be quickly and easily generated or you can choose from a library of pre-defined and graded garments. Grading can be greatly simplified, as even the most complicated calculations are carried out instantly, according to the rules you specify for your styles. AccuMark is available in two different editions, advanced and professional, according to the business' requirements or level of expertise of the team.

Images of the AccuMark program interface for designing patterns, gradings and markers for the fashion industry. This is a very useful wizard, with advanced features that allow you to create new patterns or to make changes to styles that have already been designed.

TWO NEW SOLUTIONS, ACCUMARK PDS AND ACCUMARK MTM
The AccuMark range is completed with two new products in response to the current market's new requirements. The first is AccuMark PDS, which helps to improve the quality of the work, as it designs and grades more patterns in less time, as seam allowances and grading can be automatically updated after pattern modifications. The PDS range includes the AccuMark Silhouette solution, which allows designers to manually sketch patterns on an electronic pattern table. The newly created designs are automatically displayed on screen in real-time, easing the transition between manual and computerised pattern making. The second product is AccuMark MTM (Made-to-Measure) where items are custom-made according to an individual's unique style and measurements (it can use measurements derived from 3D body scanners or tape measurements entered manually).

DIGITISING WITH ACCUMARK

To quickly and accurately input pattern pieces, the Gerber AccuMark system offers several tools, such as the Silhouette-type electronic pattern tables or those used for digitising. The digitiser workstation consists of a digitising table with a menu and a cursor. The digitiser allows you to enter information about the pattern piece. With a table of predefined grade rules as a reference, an entire range of sizes can be graded from a single base size pattern during digitising. All of the information entered into the digitiser is directly stored in the AccuMark system, where it is then ready for pattern modification or the marker or path-making process.

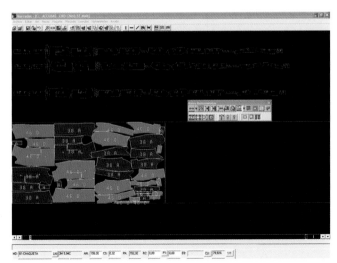 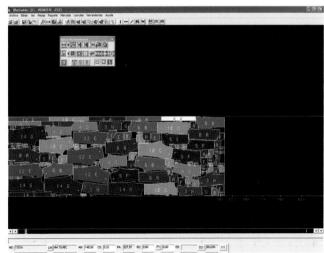

Images of the interface AccuNest Professional Edition feature, from the company Gerber Technology.

AccuNest Professional Edition is Gerber's product for efficiently and automatically creating new markers.

ULTRAQUEUE FEATURE

If you use various workstations or computers to design patterns using the AccuMark technology, you can benefit from the UltraQueue feature, which allows you to include markers from various AccuMark workstations connected to the network for automatic processing (the marker analysis is carried out by AccuNest PE) in order to improve task management by optimising your work queue. As a last point, we would like to mention that the AccuMark family and its components and optional modules require the use of a Windows XP or Vista system with a 2 GHz processor (or higher) and a minimum 1GB RAM. Should the reader have any doubts, we advise you check with technical specialists from the relevant company who will assess your needs and the optimal solutions for each case.

THE PROFESSIONAL EDITION OF THE ACCUNEST PROGRAM
Any of the AccuMark (v8.2 or higher version) options are fully compatible with AccuNest Professional Edition, Gerber's product for creating new marker layouts efficiently and automatically. The AccuNest Professional Edition (PE) program combines powerful autonesting capabilities and automatic queue management functions to maximize time and material savings. It is very easy to operate and is substantially faster and more efficient than manual marker-making, enabling you to save time and money both in sample-making and in production. AccuNest PE creates new marker layouts, analysing multiple solutions and selecting the marker with the best material utilisation. The program automatically generates nest costing and production markers to accurately calculate and optimise material use. Its layouts fit striped or checked materials, respecting piece constraints and matching lines and it also respects all pattern constraints (such as direction, rotation, tilt allowances and spread constraints) to maintain high quality standards and maximise cost-savings in the cutting room.

OPTITEX FOR AUTOMATIC PATTERN AND MARKER DESIGN

We have discussed the products offered by Gerber Technology and Lectra, and will now consider the products of the third company specialising in developing professional software for the fashion industry. OptiTex specialises in the development of innovative and easy-to-operate 2D and 3D CAD/CAM software, for textile manufacturing and other related industries. OptiTex's native Microsoft Windows-based software, for digitising, pattern engineering, grading, marking, and advanced automatic nesting, is specifically designed to meet the current needs of manufacturers of fabrics, clothing, upholstery, automotive or other related applications. The OptiTex open-architecture system is equipped with the ability to import and export multiple formats, allowing users to communicate with a wide range of software and hardware. OptiTex's "Direct Converters" are applications that read and convert Gerber and Lectra native formats, converting patterns, grading, model, and order data to the OptiTex format, while accurately retaining the original information. The converters save time by eliminating data transfer difficulties. OptiTex Direct Converters are very easy-to-use and have a fast response time so that hundreds of files are directly converted in just a few seconds. OptiTex also offers the possibility of purchasing a completely integrated CAD package including OptiTex software solutions, digitiser, and pen or ink jet plotter.

OPTITEX PATTERN DESIGN SOFTWARE (PDS)

It is easy-to-use, fast and allows all the pattern details to be kept. The digitisation of curves is easy and accurate, using only a few points. Digitisation of complicated pieces takes a few seconds and can be done at any time. The Pattern Design System (PDS) offers a powerful set of tools designed to create new patterns or edit existing ones. Movable toolbars and dialogue boxes allow each designer to create their personal working environment. Icons and tools are organised according to functionality. PDS provides features designed with clothing manufacturers in mind. Darts, seam allowance, special corners, advanced measurement techniques, pleats, complicated curves, dimension modifications and facings are all accurately adjusted.

MODULATE SYSTEM FOR CUSTOMISED PATTERNS

If you want to work with a series of particular measurements (for specific sizes or customised requirements) OptiTex offers the Modulate solution, an interactive and parametric application. Each parametric style contains a particular set of dimensions that relate to a specific person or particular manufacturing requirements. For example, a parametric jacket can be defined using dimensions called 'shoulder', 'bust', 'waist' and 'hips'. Modulate allows you to shape the jacket based on these dimensions. Any variation from changes to these parameters can be interactively visualised. Once the parametric product is fully defined by a set of dimensions, it is also ready to generate an unlimited number of different products without having to invest additional time and effort. Every variable used for a specific style can be saved in a 'Variable library' for future use. All specifications, sizes, styles and orders are saved in a standard database for repeat orders. Modulate let you visualise each step of the operation while defining the parametric model. The effect is immediately displayed on screen.

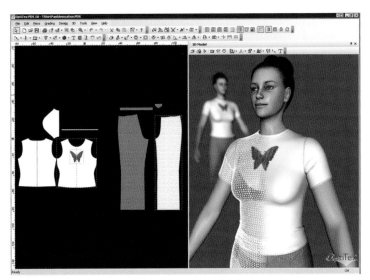

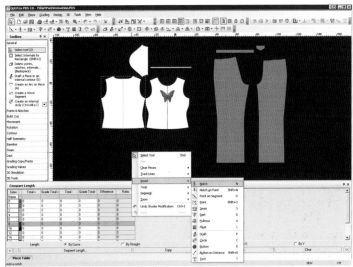

Images from the interface of the OptiTex PDS
pattern design system.

THE MARKING TOOL MATCH++

For work with designs that include *rapports* (modular repetitions), checks or stripes, Match++ is the most suitable OptiTex marking tool, which contains sophisticated matching features. The program recognises scanned or imported images and incorporates them during the marking process to optimise layout on patterns with fabric repeats. The extraordinary speed and accuracy of Match++ makes it advantageous for use in both manual and automated cutting. You can check pattern matching in the fabric before ordering it. Pre-verification allows the user to revise patterns and fabrics to ensure quality, saving time and money.

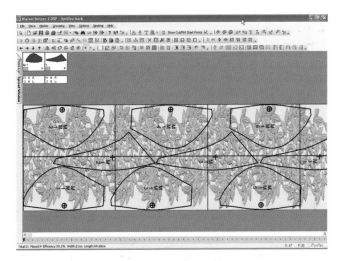

Images of the interface of the Match++ solutions

This application's features let you check pattern matching on the fabric before ordering, which minimises costs and optimises the marking task in a more precise way.

Images of the interface of the
advanced automatic nesting software Nest++2.

Like all marker-making programs its function
is to increase the use of material,
improving overall nesting and reducing
the time and labour cost.

The new tools include improvements,
aiming at greater speed and accuracy of detail,
to obtain savings in time and improved productivity.
The solutions have also developed towards specialisation.

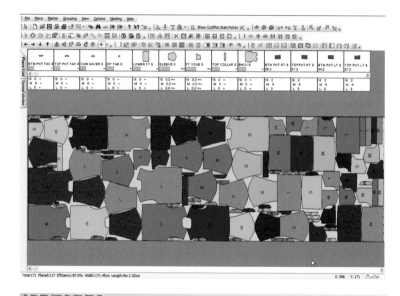

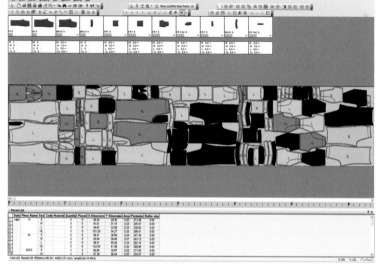

NEST++2, A POWERFUL SUPPORT SOFTWARE
OptiTex completes its product offer with the new and powerful
advanced automatic marker-making application Nest++2. The
application incorporates an intelligent algorithm that achieves
better results than those obtained manually. With Nest++2 you
can control the process time and obtain fast results. It is also
useful for obtaining precise cost proposals during price
negotiations. Nest++2 can drastically increase material
efficiency, improving overall nesting and reducing the time and
labour cost. For maximum optimisation of the work, the nesting
queue can automatically generate complete, independent,
multiple nests using unattended overnight processing.

COMPUTER MARKER-MAKING: COST AND TIME OPTIMISATION

Marking is done by computer in a way that it speeds up the process considerably, maximising the use of fabric and minimising production costs. When computer-aided cutting is implemented, the process is simplified and once the marker is fitted, following the laying, cutting is done automatically, improving quality and increasing productivity in the cutting room.

OTHER USES OF LINE DRAWING IN DESIGN AND PRODUCTION IN THE FASHION INDUSTRY

As we have mentioned before, vector drawing has another specific function within the fashion industry production process using computer-aided technology. Line drawing can be easily transferred from pattern design and marker programs to the cutting tables in the process of final preparation of designs. Again, the various companies that we have referred to as market leaders offer customised options according to needs. Given that the focus of this book is on design and not textile production, we don't need to discuss in depth the wide range of programs for the production process available on the market. However, we would like to mention that to complete our pattern design and automatic marker systems we can use:

- inkjet and pen plotters.

- automatic material laying tables (fabric, leather, plastic, etc.), which maximises the use of the material and improve the quality of the cut pieces.

- tools for matching striped, checked or patterned textiles.

- cutting machinery: on the market there are single-layer cutters (ideal for short production runs) and multi-layer cutters available in various lengths and widths to accommodate cutting requirements.

- tools for identifying cut pieces that finish the cutting process, adding information to the various cut pieces (either with labels or printing on the side of the surface) to facilitate subsequent identification.

From 2D design to virtual prototyping

In the past, the first pattern of a garment initiated successive rounds of physical prototype or sample development, each of which involved the review, adjustment and approval of a new sample. Major decisions regarding a collection often had to wait until the final samples were ready. This lengthy process lasted several weeks and required complex coordination between designers, product developers, pattern makers, marketing teams, and subcontractors. Even then, sometimes it was still difficult to consistently achieve a correct fit.

In recent years the various specialised software companies have developed tools that combine the accuracy of CAD with 3D virtual product visualisation, and provide the best existing visual simulation for virtual prototyping. The new-generation applications for virtual prototyping enhance collaboration between designers, pattern makers, product developers and marketing teams, allowing simulation and very realistic visualisation of 3D garments and their fabrics, motifs and colour ranges. The ability to visualise samples helps ensure that the original design intent and brand integrity are maintained through the production phase. Fashion professionals can increase the success of each collection, thereby improving profitability and brand image. All these solutions facilitate the transition from 2D computer-aided design (CAD) to 3D designs, with their huge simulation potential.

3D VIRTUAL PROTOTYPING TECHNOLOGY

Prototyping is a key element of the success of a collection, and 3D technology can improve performance in this phase of the textile industry. More than half the cost of a garment depends on the decisions taken during its design phase. Prototyping is, therefore, an essential stage for the success of a collection and in meeting its time, cost and quality targets.

Given that collections change continuously and product lines proliferate, ensuring a good fit has become a crucial challenge for fashion professionals. Added to this challenge is the constant pressure on the industry to reduce costs and delivery times. Customers want clothes that fit perfectly. Even if a garment is made with the best fabrics and finishes, a customer may lose interest in buying it if the fit is not perfect.

The ability to consistently ensure proper fit across collections, product lines and seasons is critical to customers' perception of the quality of the product.

When validating collections, executive committees, marketing teams and sales organisations now have virtual visual support, combined with technical data, that provide them with the complete information to make decisions and business forecasts.

Regardless of their location, they can all quickly and easily validate styles, fabrics, colour ranges, motif size and positioning, and the corresponding accessories on screen.

Virtual collection, produced with the use of 3D technology, is a support tool for helping sales teams present new collections and product ranges to points of sale and customers in the early stages of the product lifecycle. Feedback from customers and retailers can then be used to fine-tune a collection while it is still at the development phase or to eliminate products that do not appeal to buyers.

NEW 3D SYSTEMS

Virtual prototyping technology may acquire a new dimension with the introduction of new online shopping facilities, as well as a more active presence on virtual reality platforms such as Second Life, which act as powerful marketing tools. For now we will focus on 3D applications, which are not only 3D simulation mechanisms but are themselves powerful design tools, fully compatible with computer pattern design software and which can support the professional prototyping phase. Further on we will discuss the opportunities that the introduction of new three-dimensional simulation experiences has created for the distribution and communication sectors.

MODARIS 3D FIT

Modaris 3D Fit is a state-of-the-art virtual prototyping application that enhances collaboration between designers, pattern makers, product developers and marketing teams, allowing simulation and more realistic visualisation of 3D garments and their fabrics, motifs and colour ranges. First introduced at the IMB show in May 2006, Modaris 3D Fit is the result of eight years of research and development, taking advantage of Lectra's 30 years of experience serving the fashion market and its various sectors. In addition, it demonstrates Lectra's experience in the fields of measurement and 3D representation of the human body, as well as the materials used in the fashion industry. Using Modaris 3D Fit, fashion designers and pattern designers can begin to collaborate in the first stages of the process using a virtual sample. Modaris 3D Fit allows pattern designers to simulate two-dimensional patterns in three dimensions on screen and control pattern accuracy. With the help of parametric mannequins, scanned mannequins or mannequins created with other software programs, pattern designers can control the fit and proportions of the base size and all graded sizes. Lectra's parametric mannequins can be customised for a specific brand, eliminating the delay and costs associated with building wooden mannequins for different standard measurements. New measurements can be quickly visualised and realistic representations sent to all staff in the design and development chain.

VIRTUAL PROTOTYPING ALLOWS THE PRODUCT TO BE KNOWN BEFORE IT EXISTS

The introduction of the new creative and design software has emphasised the benefits for designers and manufacturers of using new technologies for virtual prototyping and other creative tools. For more than a decade, 3D design has generated a huge change in the design and manufacturing industry. However, the new-generation 3D design tools are another step towards offering designers a global concept of development. From a simple sketch of the concept, to the elevation of the sketch in a planar view, to the versatility of 3D modelling. They are aimed at designers being able to directly check the outcome of their creations, without the need for the complex physical tests that were traditionally carried out, i.e. virtual prototyping is now used to find out the exact result of a design.

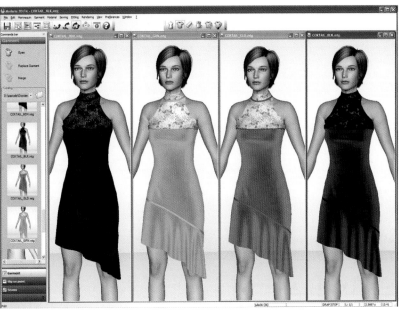

The incorporation of new technologies to pattern-making services generates multiple advantages. Using a CAD pattern-making system improves quality and increases productivity.

Virtual prototyping with Modaris 3D Fit.

Modaris 3D Fit's main benefit is that it allows pattern designers to simulate two-dimensional patterns in 3D on screen and check the pattern accuracy before finalising the design.

ABILITY TO CUSTOMISE THE PROGRAM

Modaris 3D Fit can be customised, by the Lectra technical team, in order to provide industry-specific solutions, which can range from customised virtual mannequins to the incorporation of new fabric libraries or adjustment of tools for validation and communication between different departments, ensuring a perfect fit of the programwith the company's strategy.

Modaris 3D Fit delivers realistic, highly precise views of the same garment in different materials, enabling pattern designers to assess the impact of more than 120 different fabrics and their mechanical properties. Modaris 3D Fit facilitates the development process, enabling designers and pattern designers to simulate fabrics, colours, finishes and accessories on a virtual sample. After a virtual review, the pattern designer can quickly adjust the pattern and have the physical sample produced. Using Modaris 3D Fit, the first physical sample produced conforms closely to the original creative idea and may even be the only sample required prior to production. All the technical data of each sample are included in the design itself, enabling everyone involved in the design process, pattern design, product development, and marketing processes to collaborate using current information.

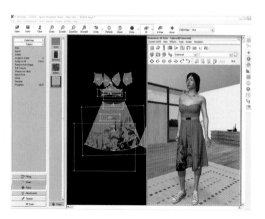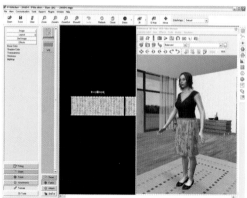

Images of the AccuMark V-Stitcher application interface. With this tool users have the possibility of transferring patterns between the two software solutions, 2D and 3D.

ACCUMARK V-STITCHER: INTEGRATION OF 2D TECHNOLOGY WITH 3D SIMULATION

AccuMark V-Stitcher is the new pattern design product offered in the Gerber Technology range, which has been created in partnership with Browzwear Ltd. (www.browzwear.com), an expert in 3D applications for the fashion industry.

A single software interface allows AccuMark users to exchange patterns between the two software solutions, 2D and 3D. This allows the pattern data to be developed in AccuMark and directly viewed in V-Stitcher (in the same way, you can modify these patterns in V-Stitcher and effortlessly transfer them to AccuMark). The modifications are also transferred to the 3D virtual mannequin in real-time. With this new application, realistic representations can be created, simulating the texture, draping and fit of the garments to display them on a virtual model based on the pattern data you have chosen, with fabric and texture. Our virtual garments are generated from two-dimensional patterns and are displayed on 3D mannequins to achieve an exact fit. Your collection can have an unlimited number of virtual mannequins.

TWO SIMULATORS: V-STYLER AND C-ME

The AccuMark V-Stitcher range can be completed with two software solutions, V-Styler and C-Me, that are also the result of their partnership with Browzwear Ltd. The first, V-Styler allows designers to realistically simulate the drape of fabric on a 3D garment, as well as enabling the detailed creation of virtual samples. C-Me is a viewer that allows remote display of collections and cooperative fit and design sessions. It is especially designed for sharing collections with buyers, suppliers and retailers at any point in the process of pre-production, production or communication.

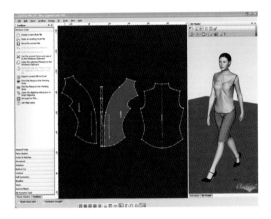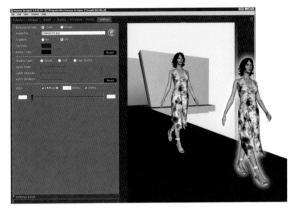

Images of the 3D Runway interface,
OptiTex's 3D prototyping solution.

3D RUNWAY, OPTITEX'S 3D MODELLING SYSTEM

3D Runway is a garment-simulation system based on accurate CAD pattern details and accurate information on real fabric characteristics. The OptiTex 3D Runway suite of tools uses a natural combination of two-dimensional models or patterns with state-of-the-art 3D technology, offering a complete integration with OptiTex's pattern design programs, PDS and Modulate (which we have discussed previously).

3D Runway virtually produces garments with easy-to-use tools, enabling the creation of a wide range of simulations at early design stages (it analyses fabric behaviour, proof-fitting assumptions, etc.) so that realistic results are obtained throughout the process of creation of the garment, without having to wait for completion of the design creation process. This means that the program shows at all times the different stages in the creation of the 'virtual prototype', in a realistic and easy-to-visualise way (the classic 3D modelling programs contain very complex views, in which only an expert can sense what the object will look like after rendering).

3D Runway Creator enables the models included in the program to be 'dressed', alternatively you can opt to create a customised model with your own parametric information. The virtual parametric mannequins provided by the application are highly adjustable to more than 40 body measurements, saving a great deal of time in size-testing. The fabric movement simulator included in OptiTex 3D Runway takes OptiTex 3D technology to the next level, allowing Runway users to incorporate complex processes of fabric collisions, intersections and motion capabilities, to a file that can then be displayed or sent out to non-OptiTex users. Adding motion to the model is very easy – a user can run the preinstalled motion capture files or import them from another third-party application. A model with movement simulation is no longer a static image, but offers the possibility to visualise the pattern in everyday situations, thereby increasing the realism of our designs. Yoram Burg, President OptiTex USA. UU. defines the motion simulator incorporated in the program as follows:

'This new and highly accurate fabric motion simulator extends OptiTex capabilities and allows our users, from the first design, to move to full motion of the pattern all within one suite of products and within one application. Your entire design process can now be created within OptiTex's large variety of software solutions.'

3D graphics for fashion design

3D graphics are especially useful for any designer, increasing the repertoire of available resources as well as often being the simplest way to obtain the desired image. The term 3D computer graphics refers to graphic artwork created with the aid of computers and specialised 3D software.

The design of 3D graphics covers several phases of development, the first of which is modelling. This phase consists of shaping individual objects which are then later used in the scene. There are various types of geometry to work with in this phase: NURBS (Non-Uniform Rational B-Splines), geometry-based modelling and polygonal modelling (or subdivision surfaces).

NURBS are mathematical representations of 3D geometry that can accurately describe any shape from simple lines, circles, arcs or curves, to the most complex 3D organic free-form surface or solid. Because of their flexibility and accuracy, NURBS models can be used in any process from illustration to manufacturing. The amount of information required for a NURBS representation of a geometric shape is much smaller than that required by common faceted approximations. The subdivision surface is a method of representing a smooth surface by the specification of a polygon mesh. This process takes the mesh and subdivides it, creating new vertices and faces while each polygonal face is divided into smaller areas that better approximate to the desired surface. Once we have modelled our design, we move to the phases of texturing and lighting, which control the incidence of light, combining with textures. Designs generated with 3D modellings can be animated with basic transformations in the three axes (rotation, scale and translation). The last phase of work is rendering.

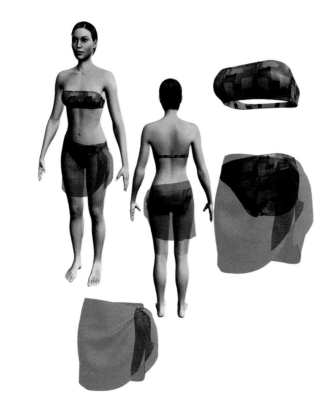

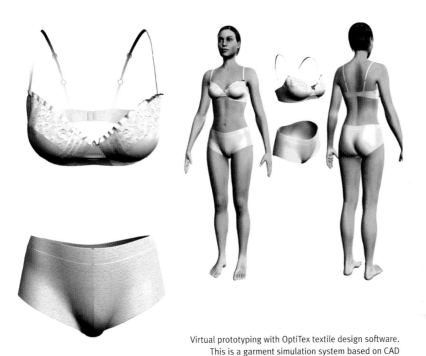

Virtual prototyping with OptiTex textile design software. This is a garment simulation system based on CAD patterns and real fabric characteristics. Designers and pattern makers can visualise any pattern modification in 3D.

RENDERING

When working with a 3D computer design program, it is not normally possibly to visualise the desired final scene in real time. As it is more complex, it requires too high a computational power, therefore the 3D environment is created with a simpler form of visualisation and the slow process of rendering is generated later to achieve the desired end results. The rendering time depends largely on the material and lighting parameters that are established. Normally each 3D application has its own rendering engine, however there are also plug-ins (add-ons that are associated with another main application to add a new and generally very specific function) which make the calculation within the program using special formulas. The compatibility with different rendering engines and the speed are probably the most important elements of the new professional applications, which practically allow us to visualise in real time in our 3D model any change that we make in any of the design parameters (so that the design is much more agile and visual at all times).

3D MODELLING

There are so many applications designed for 3D modelling that it is impossible to mention them all in this book. Nevertheless, we will name a few of the most popular, which are Maya, Softimage, 3D Studio Max, Blender, Rhinoceros, LightWave, POV-ray and Houdini.

All of them incorporate significant innovations in their tools for 'texturing' and 'illuminating' three-dimensional objects to simulate hyperrealistic representation. Most 3D design applications include the possibility of animating the elements in a given space. The main industries which work with these programs are the more technical areas of industrial design, computer game companies, architectural practices or engineering companies. There are few 3D modellers specifically adapted to the fashion industry, although advanced users of any of the programs can use them perfectly in any professional field. The add-ons designed for more general-purpose programs include plugs-in for 3D Studio Max, Clothes Reyes (www.reyesinfografica.com) or SimCloth (www.spot3d.com/simcloth).

Both allow an improved simulation of the effects of gravity, weight, transparency and overlapping layers of fabric in 3D creations (especially when animating them). These effects are best and most frequently used by the video games creation industry. However, we are beginning to observe an enormous interest in them in the fashion business due to their high simulation capabilities. There are some areas within the fashion industry that are leaders in the implementation of 3D design services. Probably jewellery and footwear design are the most representative within this new generation. In recent years, specific applications and plug-ins have emerged with highly effective solutions for these areas of design and creation. Within these fashion-specific solutions, the most notable are the plug-ins of the general program Rhinoceros (although they can work as separate programs), RhinoGold and RhinoShoe, for the design of jewellery and footwear respectively, and the 3Design application also for designing jewellery. All these applications are having a wide impact on the industry as well as the educational systems of many fashion training schools. In this book we prefer to emphasise those programs developed specifically for the fashion industry, whilst remembering that many of their functions can be obtained from other more all-purpose programs.

Virtual prototyping using OptiTex 3D technology.

ABOUT PLUG-IN MODULES

Plug-in modules are programs developed by software developers working in conjunction with the main software company, which add features to this software. Almost all the design programs include a number of importing, exporting and special-effects plug-ins, which are automatically installed in the subfolders of the Plug-in folder of each application.

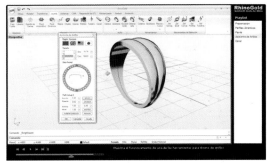

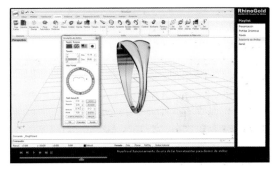

RHINOGOLD

RhinoGold (www.rhinogold.com) is the new specific jewellery-design solution based on the technology of the Rhinoceros 4.0 NURBS 3D modeller for Windows. RhinoGold only runs on Windows 2000, XP Pro, XP Home and Vista. It can also work in Intel Mac operating systems but only those with BootCamp or Parallels (these applications enable you to install and work in a Windows environment from a Mac computer). This program is easy-to-use and very flexible. Its menu still offers all the Rhinoceros' design options, but adds a new toolbar with specific jewellery-design functions. In this way, the program enables advanced users to take advantage of all of Rhinoceros' 3D design technology (the general 3D modelling program), whereas beginners can just use the specific RhinoGold tools for the jewellery field without needing to use the rest of the functions. One of its main advantages is that it allows you to preview the function of the 3D modelling tools without losing time in the rendering process, as the application includes basic and real time rendering, all compatible with other solutions such as Flamingo, Penguin, Vray and Brazil, etc.

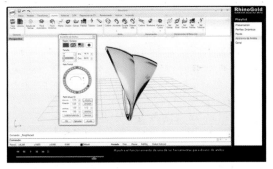

Images of the RhinoGold application interface showing the operation of one of the tools for designing rings using wizards.
www.tdmsolutions.com

Images from the RhinoGold program interface, with a review of its main functions (gem studio, wizard for rings and chains, automatic and dynamic pavé, solutions for creating channels and scaling rings, etc.

RhinoGold makes it possible for jewellery designers and manufacturers to design, modify and manufacture jewellery completely, quickly and precisely without sacrificing a clear and intuitive interface (which both simplifies and reduces learning time). Its easy operation allows designers to exercise precise control. The language used in the interface is the usual jewellery terminology, facilitating clear communication between professionals in the industry. Like all the other 3D modelling programs, it includes tools for 2D drawing or 3D modelling, updating the information in each of the scenarios that are selected.

Its tools are adapted to the specific needs of the jewellery sector and greatly assist the task of creation of an piece, simplifying the most common work process functions. As jewellery design is characterised by high levels of accuracy, the program includes tools for analysing the weight of metals and gems, annotations (to obtain all the necessary technical details of the piece and improve communication with the prototyping or production teams) and CAM tools (to obtain the necessary technical information to directly transmit the design to a milling machine for wax prototyping) or the STL repair function (that allows you to create reliable STL files for 3D wax printers).

JEWELLERY DESIGN

Pavé is the term used by jewellers to refer to the encrusting of gems across a base surface, normally set in a grid layout. The word is so common in jewellery design that the name has been given to the program tools.

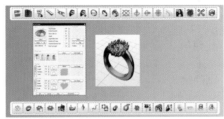

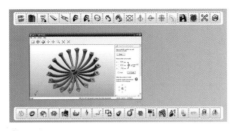

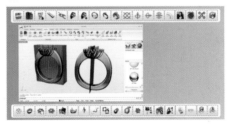

STL FILE

STL is the standard file format for rapid prototyping. This type of file uses a mesh of small triangles on the surfaces in order to define the shape of the object. Stereolithography files (.stl) were conceived as a simple way to store information about 3D objects. The main use of .stl archives is physical prototyping based on designs which are computer-generated or on processed 3D data. Almost all modern 3D software packages support direct export to STL with varying levels of control. Some allow you to select the density of the exported .stl file (the number of polygons defining the solid), while others only offer the option of selecting the name of the file and ascii/binary options. For an object defined in a .stl file to be correctly constructed, the triangles should fit together perfectly, without any gaps or overlaps. The .stl format is a standard output format for most CAD programs, and the number of triangles to be used can be previously defined by the user. 3D modelling programs rarely work on .stl files and it is normally necessary to export models to this format before beginning 3D printing. Given the differences between .stl format and the original 3D formats, conversions tend to leave structural faults in the model. Therefore, .stl files must be checked using special software before being used to manufacture a model. The 'STL Repair Assistant' in RhinoGold can optimise the file.

3DESIGN

3Design (www.3design.com) is another specific software for the design and manufacture both of jewellery pieces and accessories. It is the result of hard work backed up by over 15 years experience in the jewellery industry, working with firms as prestigious as Cartier and Dupont, which shows that the product has emerged as a result of broad and in-depth knowledge of the industry. The software is compatible with the different platforms currently used today, PC, Mac and Linux, and is developed on Java SystemWeb Server, and therefore it is constantly updated via the Internet by downloading the latest available version. In addition, any design that is already created can be built into a personal library to be used at a later date as a component of future creations.

The most outstanding feature of 3Design is its parametric structure and its commands designed for specific jewellery-design tasks.

In parametric software, any action or modification that we make is stored in the parametric tree, which means that the design can be modified at any stage of its creation without having to do a complete redesign. Changes can thus be included quickly and easily. With a base design, corrections can be made to obtain a comprehensive collection based on a few designs. 3Design is set up to make photorealistic presentations of designs and display 3D creations in a professional manner. It is also the only software on the market that, throughout the design phase, represents a gem with the colour of its metal and not as a representation of its shape. This function allows designers to enhance their creations: to modify the various colours of the metal or piece as they wish, adding shading, transparency or special light effects to the object created, i.e., reproduce a complete scenario for the designed piece with shine and polish.

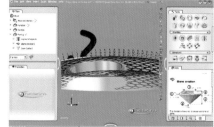
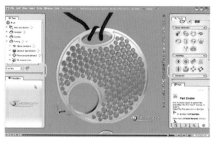
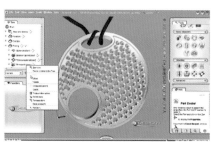
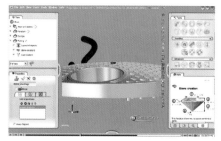

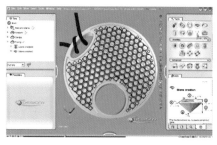

Images from the 3Design program interface showing the use of some of its tools for creating pieces of jewellery.

Images of rendering for presenting work with the 3Design application.

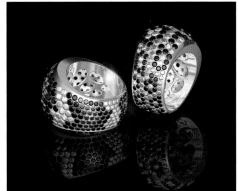

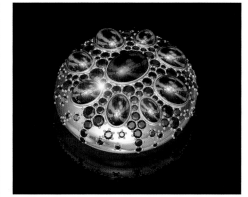

SURFACES AND SHADING

The application also allows you to work with surfaces (for designers who have experience with it). Working with surfaces is just as simple as working with 3D solids, instantly creating cylinders, boxes, toruses and spheres. The high-quality shading of 3Design enables accurate previewing of the design with a greater appearance of volume. The powerful shading represents, from the beginning, creation with the material you are going to use, whether that is gold, silver, diamond, emerald, etc. Work is always with a real 3D object and not just a representation of a model.

In the production phase, creating the design in 3D has the advantage that, by using the rapid prototyping technology, masters can be obtained for the production process. The advantages of this method are speed and accuracy. Moreover, with a just one ring the full range of sizes can be created and produced in a few hours. 3Design offers many import formats including the BMP image format, so that you can take designs on paper, scan them and begin to build the 3D model with the projections of the sketches.

3D printing technology

Designers, engineers and architects need to visualise the work they do on the computer with real models that they can touch and handle. Traditionally, prototypes were used for this visualisation, which were manufactured models, laborious and very costly to produce. Until very recently, the idea was inconceivable of sending 3D data generated with a CAD program directly to a machine capable of 'printing' a real model in cross-sections, as if it were a home printer.

3D printers use two basic components for 'printing' rapid prototypes: a special substance (similar to talcum powder) known as a 'composite', and an ink that has the property of compressing the composite. The 'powder' that the 3D printer uses as a printing medium has various properties and can be used to directly make colour models. To produce moulds or inverse moulds, elastic (rubber-based) parts can be made and parts that can be fitted together.

USUAL TYPES OF COMPOSITE

- HIGH-DEFINITION COMPOSITE: is the standard material for strong, high-definition parts. It is the preferred material for printing both 'plaster colour' and 'full colour' as well as maximising the surface finish, resolution and strength of the part.

- INVESTMENT OR LOST WAX CASTING COMPOSITE: based on cellulose, special fibres and additives to provide accurate parts that can absorb the wax and minimise residue during the burn-out process.

- GRAVITY DIE CASTING COMPOSITE: Material for printing gravity die casting moulds for non-ferrous metals, based on foundry sand, plaster and additives to provide strong moulds with a good surface finish and that can withstand the heat required for casting.

- 'SNAP-FIT' SPECIAL COMPOSITE: material optimised for infiltration with Z-Snap™ epoxy, for parts with flexible properties.

- 'ELASTOMERIC' SPECIAL COMPOSITE: material optimised for infiltration with an elastomer, perfect for parts with stretch properties such as rubber. The material base consists of cellulose, special fibres and additives to provide accurate parts capable of absorbing the elastomer.

Work produced by the goldsmith Joan Codina
using three-dimensional design techniques.
www.codinaorfebres.com

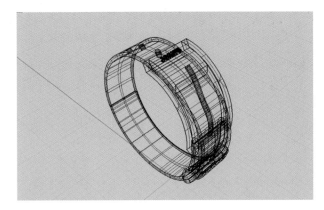

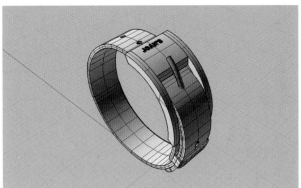

ADVANTAGES OF 3D PRINTING

3D printing technology differs from other rapid prototyping methods (such as the creation of models through plastic injection) in several fundamental points. Firstly, it can create full-colour models thanks to the combined effect of the four inkjet heads (magenta, cyan, yellow and black). Colour distribution is extremely accurate and allows models to be labelled with text (design annotations, labels, etc.), reproduce brands, colour areas to differentiate them, etc. Models are printed in full colour, without the need for laborious further processing.

Secondly, the time to finish a piece varies according to its size and complexity, but in all cases 3D printing is the fastest prototyping technology on the market (between five and ten times faster than any other solution). Moreover, multiple separate prototypes can be printed simultaneously to take advantage of the entire printing surface.

When printing is finished and the model is complete, the excess composite is vacuumed and recycled for future use, leaving the model clean and free of residue. At this stage in the process, the part is still fragile and should be handled with care. To give it the final finish, it must be infiltrated (dipped) in one of the various special adhesive infiltrates that increases the hardness and strength of the prototype part until it can be handled without any special precautions. The printing materials are cheaper than those of other rapid prototyping solutions, making 3D printers well-suited to continuous production environments. This machine is capable of producing quality models with a high market value and an extremely low production cost. With other solutions, prototyping is reserved for the later stages of the design process or even for the final presentation to the client. The reduced cost of the technology allows models to be produced at various intermediate stages of the design process.

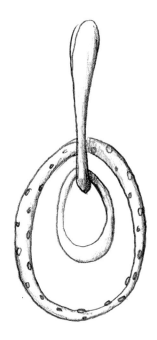

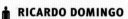

RICARDO DOMINGO

He currently manages his own studio with a multidisciplinary team of designers, as a creative director and consultant in art, design and image for businesses in the jewellery industry.

His clients include Antonio Puig perfumes, Cunill Orfebres, the Christian Bernard group (Oro Vivo), the Cadarso group (Geresa) Noah Barcelona, Madreperla, Unión Suiza, Joy Taker and the art direction of the jewellery of Agatha Ruiz de la Prada, Toni Miró, Adolfo Domínguez, Victorio & Lucchino, etc.

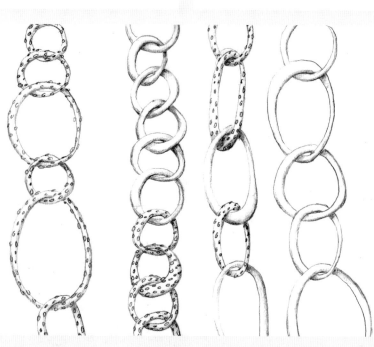

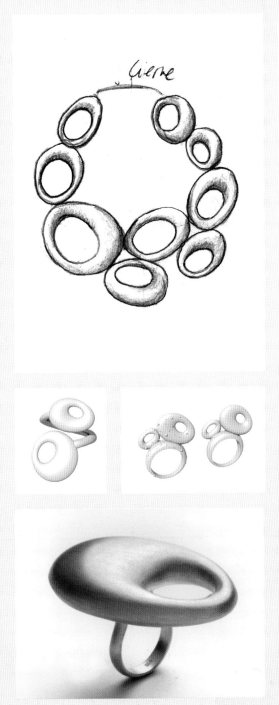

The project we include here was commissioned by
Oscar Figueroa, CEO of the firm d'Escorcia, a
silver jewellery company in Tasco, Mexico. Oscar Figueroa
entrusted Ricardo Domingo's studio with the
implementation of his new project. Oscar Figueroa Jewels
was launched with an impeccable, carefully studied
image and some very well-crafted pieces.
During the creation of the collection,
Ricardo Domingo's team started the initial sketches
for the entire collection, passing immediately
to the final stages of design both in 2D and in
3D, to bring out the final prototypes that can be
seen in the pictures. The designs move between
tradition and modernity, craftsmanship and technology.

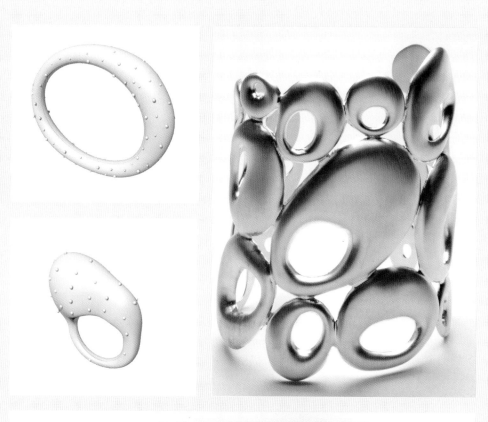

Ricardo Domingo's jewellery design studio
has always tried to stay at the forefront of the industry's
technological innovations in tools for optimising their
work.

The jewellery segment, taking into account the enormous
impact of the costs of the raw material itself, has
managed to adapt the innovative resources to improve
their work process without losing its enormous
creative skill. Jewellery generated with 3D technology, as
we have seen earlier, can pass straight to '3D printers'
to create the final moulds, greatly facilitating
the transition from design to the final prototype.

Furthermore, all the technical information
stored in the computing solutions facilitates the
manufacturing process up to the final
production of the parts.

PROJECT Oscar Figueroa Jewels
ART DIRECTOR Ricardo Domingo
JEWELLERY DESIGN Mireia Rossell,
Óscar Figueroa and Ricardo Domingo
2D Julia Ribera
3D Joan Codina
GRAPHIC DESIGN Anna Sánchez

AND COM

MARKETING
MUNICATION

Conveying a concept

The fashion industry does not only design and manufacture clothing, footwear, jewellery or accessories. All the products also go through the machinery of management, distribution, promotion and communication which puts them in touch with the final consumer. The new computing media have revolutionised the way tasks and work phases are conceived. The widespread use of the Internet, international management of production/distribution and the emergence of the new Web 2.0 and its emphasis on user participation in the communication process are some of the key concepts for understanding this chapter.

Collection management

The new era has brought major changes to product lifecycle management. It is not enough to speed up the processes. Nor is it sufficient to reduce costs. The change requires businesses in the fashion industry to rethink their strategies for marketing, design, planning, product development, engineering, sourcing and manufacturing processes. The new PLM systems integrate all the phases of the product life cycle, allowing manufacturers closer control of the processes and the critical inter-relationships that determine the growth and profitability of brands.

The PLM (Product Lifecycle Management) functions have a similar approach to knowledge management, but focusing on the product. In other words, the objective of the PLM is to allow the various company departments, from production to sales, to share knowledge of the different stages in the lifecycle of a product (design, manufacturing, storage, transport, sale, after-sales service, recycling).

The PLM approach requires close cooperation within the company to gather the information related to the product manufacturing stages, as well as the tools for managing customer and supplier relationships. These PLM solutions enable companies to manage the entire lifecycle of their collections and products, and reduce the delays and costs associated with product design, besides providing a important support for decision-making, rationalising and improving the product development processes, and the synchronisation and traceability of the information flows. The tools integrated in the PLM solutions allow those responsible for decision-taking to be fully aware of all the development, offering them an overview of the simultaneous processes while reducing or eliminating the inefficient steps when operating in a global environment. Therefore, PLM solutions greatly optimise the different types of collaboration between contractors and suppliers. Brands and distributors often outsource all or part of the development and engineering phases and retain the processes of innovation and quality control. Outsourcing can be organised with local suppliers or relocated, enabling cost-reductions.

PLM platforms are normally 100% web-based, with standards that support global deployment and allow visibility, control, collaboration and assistance in decision-making throughout the product lifecycle. They operate from a server and the information can be accessed from anywhere in the world using only a computer with an Internet connection and a browser. Product specifications and images can be created or modified somewhere in the world and be viewed in real time somewhere else. This ease of access is essential in the world of fashion, in which companies sometimes have hundreds of partners and suppliers spread across the five continents. In order to secure data access and ensure that only strictly necessary information is disseminated outside, user profiles and access rights can be easily and tightly defined.

There are currently two big packages with professional PLM management tools that are specifically geared to the fashion industry. Lectra (www.lectra.com) offers LectraFashionPLM, a package adaptable to the needs of each business and which is fully compatible with the garment design and pattern-making, marking and virtual prototyping applications referred to in previous chapters. Gerber Technology's parallel product (www.gerbertechnology.com) is Fashion Lifecycle Management (FLM), which increases its WebPDM's data management capabilities into a robust, company-wide tool to improve and manage the product development process on a global basis.

Both products, produced by the leading companies in the development of specific software for the fashion industry, adapt to their clients' needs by way of a team of specialised consultants and technical experts who ensure the best advice for rationalising the organisation (even during the process of change) and the implementation of new tools, fully synchronised to avoid management problems.

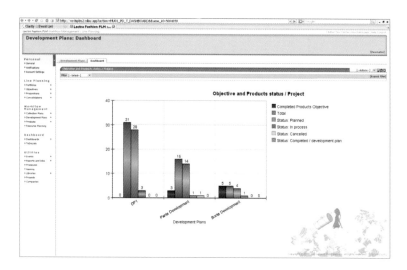

Images from the LectraFashionPLM interface, a package adaptable to the needs of each company and fully compatible with applications for clothing design, pattern-making, marking, and virtual prototyping.

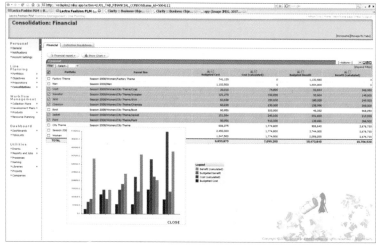

TOOLS FOR PRODUCT MANAGEMENT AT THE POINT OF SALE

When the product reaches the point of sale, new needs arise, such as product management in the warehouse (by colours and sizes), distribution, invoicing, automated management of product bar codes, the issue of receipts, vouchers, and transfers to other outlets and invoices. There are particular applications that can help by providing integrated solutions that can be adapted to our needs. One of the most popular packages is NaviWear, based on Microsoft-Navision technology (www.es.tectura.com), capable of providing specific solutions to the wholesale textile distribution sector, chains of shops and manufacturers, managing everything related to sizes, colours, seasons, etc. Byte Factory (www.bytefactory.es) offers the solutions WinTextil, WinMulti and WinTPV in order to adapt better to the client according to the type of business. Other firms that also offer general tools are Odacash (www.odacash.com) and Quasars (www.quasars.es).

Visual merchandising

Visual merchandising is the way in which a brand presents its product and advertising material at its retail outlets. It is aimed at creating an image with which the public can identify it. A balanced combination of product display and advertising, along with a defined look for window displays, produces a solid image of what is represented.

Visual merchandising is what ultimately seduces the customer into buying a product. It is the last strategic link of a chain aimed at obtaining this purchase. This chain includes research and product development, production and distribution, marketing and advertising. To obtain greater sales opportunities, it is essential to know the basic principles of customer purchasing behaviour. The shop, showroom or trade show stand must represent the image that the company wants to project, interpret the way it operates and adapt to the customer's needs. It must be functional and effective. Current techniques are not longer limited to decorating window displays and placing mannequins in the display areas – the scope of designers' contributions are now only bound by their own imagination and the resources at their disposal. An ever-increasing number of companies and businesses work with companies specialising in visual merchandising. Displays need to be coordinated with advertising and other promotional sales tools in order to achieve maximum effectiveness. Just as it is clear that the collections that are offered to the different audiences change continually, the environment where they are exhibited and put on sale must also change, since the public, onlookers and buyers build up an image of the company when they pass through these places. In such a competitive market as the current one, it not enough just to display products or to provide a comfortable sales environment; it is necessary and advisable to take advantage of all the visual design resources so that both the products and the settings are as attractive as possible. This largely depends on those in charge of visual merchandising at the shop or company and their collaborators (interior designers, shop window dressers and shop furniture designers).

Shop window designs for Custo Barcelona in various international locations.
© Miguel Caballero and Federica Sandretti.

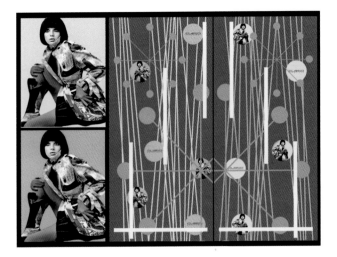

SOME SIMPLE TRICKS TO INFLUENCE PURCHASE DECISIONS

Starting with the front door, if we can locate it on the right of the premises we can ensure that the customer goes around the whole the store and thereby we increase the likelihood of purchase. The shop window is a key factor – it must draw attention, be original and have clear ideas. Experts say that the number of products in a shop window is inversely proportional to the impression of quality. In the shop's interior, a customer comes in with an idea (or with no idea) and ends up impulse-buying. To encourage this, the shop must locate featured products at strategic points. The most well-known brands (for multi-brand companies) often work to catch your eye, and the products that are placed on their right are more successful. The shop entrance, the central passageway and the cash-desk areas are the key areas in a shop. In the first, the customer is trapped with offers so that they don't leave; the second will have the greatest transit of people, and in the third, where the queues are formed, the consumer is exposed to a wait in which they can continue shopping.

Furniture design for the Custo Barcelona corner
of the duty-free shop in Madrid airport.
© Miguel Caballero and Federica Sandretti.

Stand and visual design for
Colcci at the Bread and Butter
Barcelona tradeshow, Summer 07.
© Miguel Caballero and Federica Sandretti.

Furniture design for the Custo Barcelona corner
of the duty-free shop in Madrid airport.
© Miguel Caballero and Federica Sandretti.

AutoCAD

Autocad is probably the software most widely-used by professionals in work related to spatial representation, such as interior or furniture design. Part of the AutoCAD program is designed for producing plans, using traditional graphic drawing tools (colour, line thickness and dithering textures). AutoCad, from version 11 onwards, uses the concept of model space and paper space to separate design and drawing phases in 2D and 3D. The AutoCAD file extension is .dwg, although it allows exporting to other formats, of which the best-known is .dxf. It also works with IGES and STEP formats to manage compatibility with other drawing software. Currently, the latest version of AutoCAD is AutoCAD 2009. Like other computer-assisted design programs, AutoCAD has a database of geometric entities (points, lines, arcs, etc.) which are used through a drawing editor in a graphic display. User interaction takes place through editing or drawing commands from the command line, to which the program is primarily orientated. Modern versions of the program allow these to be introduced through a graphic interface, which automates the process. Like all CAD programs, it processes vector-type images, although it allows photographic files (or bitmaps) to be incorporated, where basic or primitive figures are drawn (lines, arcs, rectangles, texts, etc.), and using editing tools, more complex graphics are created. The program lets you organise the objects by means of layers or strata, ordering the drawing into separate parts with different colour and graphics. The drawing of series of objects is managed through the use of blocks, which allows multiple identical objects to be defined and modified simultaneously.

E-commerce: the Internet as a sales platform

In recent years a new player has emerged among marketing tools, which is e-commerce. It can be defined as a form of transaction or interchange of commercial information based on data transmission, using communication networks such as the Internet.

E-commerce includes not only buying and selling but all the activities leading up to it, such as marketing, the search for information, prior contracting, etc. Today the greatest use of Internet is for advertising; businesses mainly use the Internet to gain recognition, to offer products and services and attract new customers. Companies that are attracted by the idea that what is published on the Internet will be able to be seen from anywhere in the world, make the use of e-commerce go far beyond mere advertising. Therefore, e-commerce represents a new type of trade that has emerged as a direct consequence of new technologies. This network of networks enables trade to have a global scope, or at least that is its intention.

If the Internet has become a virtual shop window of businesses advertising their products and offers to other companies and consumers, at the time of purchase too many buyers end up resorting to traditional commercial means. However, analysing the rapid development of new technologies over the past ten years, it is not unreasonable to think that within a short time electronic commerce will predominate in all types of transactions. To complete the purchase, the virtual point of sale (POS) terminal or payment gateway offers the solution for those companies that operate with their customers via the Internet to collect payment. It is the same service as charging through a credit card in a physical shop. When a customer makes an online purchase, confirms their order and proceeds to payment, the application takes them to the bank's website. This is a simple procedure which involves completing a form that requests the card numbers, which are sent in a totally secure way to the bank server, where the appropriate checks are made on the bank balance and passwords.

FREUTAG'S F-CUT
One of the cornerstones of the Freutag fashion accessories brand is the individuality of its parts (created with tarpaulins from different lorries). This is achieved through the F-cut application in which the consumer directly becomes the designer. The application, launched a few years ago, allows you to design your own bag through a relatively simple menu on the website, and also purchase it through the same web format.

Once the payment process has been completed, the online store is notified whether the payment has been successfully made. The POS system is safe for making payment via the Internet both for the buyer and the seller, and is the most widespread formula among online consumers. Nowadays all banks offer this service. The information that is exchanged online is encrypted and guarantees the security of it not being accessible or manipulable.

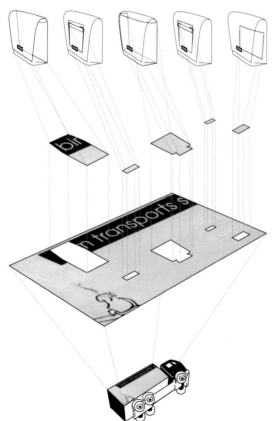

F-cut is very simple, but the final responsibility
for the design is not the brand's but ours.
The service provides help with all the phases of
the design of the item, but with a significant capacity for
decision-making and customisation.

www.freitag.ch/f-cut

One of Privalia.com's most recent projects has
been to open its space to the new Web 2.0
ideas. The Privalia blog will be launched
soon, offering information on trends and
products as well as creating a space in which
members can express themselves, make
suggestions and interact.

PRIVALIA.COM

Privalia.com is a private club that organises specific single-label sales through the Internet, only of top brands, at exceptional prices and exclusively for its members. It was launched in June 2006 in Barcelona, but has grown rapidly; since December 2007 it also operates on the Italian market, and as from November 2008 it will be launched on the Brazilian market.

In Spain it has carried out more than 700 campaigns, and collaborates on an ongoing basis with the leading fashion and sports brands closest to its target:

SPORTS: Nike, Adidas, O'Neil, New Balance, Umbro, Champion, Merrell, etc.

FASHION: Diesel, Adolfo Dominguez, Pedro del Hierro, Guess, Jordi Labanda, Paramita, etc.

ACCESSORIES: Breil, D&G, Lupo, Tous, Seiko, etc.

It has 800,000 active registered users and over 160,000 individual buyers. The number of purchase orders processed each month now exceeds 50,000. Use of the online sales services is increasing. Consumers have lost their initial fear and are satisfied with the opportunities that this service offers. Privalia describes its buyers as individuals who use the Internet regularly for making orders and other services.

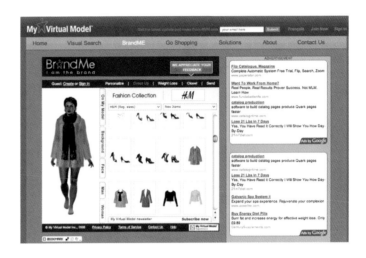

One of the major advances introduced by fashion companies are virtual dressing rooms. They allow the user to access a large number of garments simply by entering their measurements and their sizes. The result is the same as if they had tried them on directly.

VIRTUAL DRESSING ROOM

The fashion industry has its own particular needs that need to be built into online platforms. One of the main problems relates to solving the management of garment sizes and fitting. Studies show that over 30% of clothing bought online is returned, mainly due to problems with the fit. One of the new technology tools being developed to minimise this problem is the 'Virtual Dressing Room'. This type of application converts the consumer in a virtual model, so they can visualise how the selected garment will look. The dressing room also offers the possibility of being suggested outfits from the available items. Most of these programs require the consumer to enter a series of data and measurements (between 5 and 32 measurements, depending on the accuracy of the program) in order to build virtually a parametric model as close as possible to the original (websites offer instructions and examples for the necessary measurements). Other applications use the 'digitisation' of the model based on a photograph or a three-dimensional scan. This is a much more accurate process but highly complex; however the program uses the measurements from consumer bases to improve its ability to adapt to future re-creations. Some companies carry out scanner campaigns to store their customers' data and thus facilitate the shopping they can do online. To give just one example, EZsize recently installed a body scanner in the Best-Fit area of the Saks Fifth Avenue shop in New York City. With all this information, a virtual rendering of the model will be produced, creating a 'cyber mannequin', a virtual model of that person in 3D. Using a customised mannequin, consumers can then go shopping online with the certainty of getting the right size. Some systems even warn you, using areas of colour, about potential fit problems (garments that are too short or too narrow). There is the option of rotating the cyber mannequin to gain a front, back, and profile view, and using a zoom to enlarge specific sections and examine details.

One of the main challenges of the various companies offering these services is to optimise the rendering time to avoid long and tedious waits. As most of these tools are installed on the Web, they rely heavily on the speed of data flows and the capacity of the user or consumer's computer. There is a wide range of re-creations of virtual models on the market linked to this sector, to name a few, C-me created by Browzwear Vtryon and EZsize, both solutions from EZsize, The Right Size, or Virtual Fashion, a division of the Spanish company Reyes Infográfica. However, the solution that has been most greatly developed in recent years is the My Virtual Model tool (created by My Virtual Model Inc.). There is a long list of international clients who have decided to incorporate it into their websites.

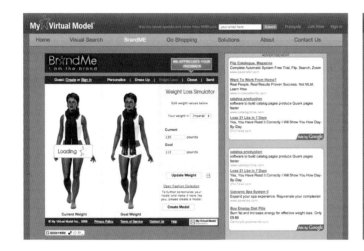

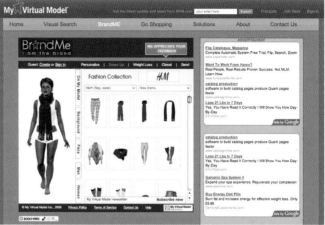

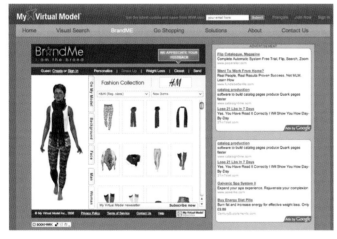

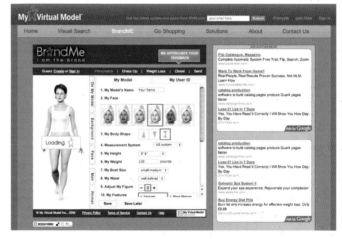

BRANDME

BrandME is the new tool offered by My Virtual Model Inc., with improved features for developing efficient marketing and communication with their customers. BrandME aims to convert and unify the 'virtual identity' with the idea of social relations and the shopping experience, allowing new means of communication between the consumer and the brand. From BrandME, not only can virtual 3D models be created (adding your face from a photograph), but it also allows interaction with the collection on sale, making suggestions, giving outfit ideas and sharing the final results with virtual communities or 'friends' in blogs (Facebook, MySpace, etc.). All the user's information is stored in their profile, giving the company first-hand information about favourite looks or successful garment combinations. By enabling the sharing of part of the information, free advertising is generated in other areas of the Internet.

Fashion in the new virtual world

Fashion has also found its place in this parallel 'virtual' world, a paradise where thousands of companies have already started making their fortune and in which each day over a million euros change hands. Why shouldn't virtual characters be able to window shop at the most powerful fashion companies and chains? Some of these even have their own island (the geography of Second Life is divided into different virtual islands).

The virtual world also has some areas set aside for fashion; Belladona Island is a fantasy location where some luxury shops have recently appeared. Located on the islet of the Italian magazine Style, it is a futuristic space where top brands have presented their clothes collections. The experience of buying clothes in Second Life seems very interesting. Undoubtedly, one of the obstacles that online fashion shopping has always had to overcome is the coldness of the purchasing process, very remote from the traditional sale. The enormous simulation potential of Second Life could overturn this handicap. Similarly, the Spanish Inditex group brands have also opened their doors in Second Life. Some items of these brands (jewellery, accessories) which appear dotted all over the island. In this sense the virtual space is simply a niche for brand advertising. In Second Life you can also find companies who design and sell fashion products exclusively in the virtual environment (they do not have a reference point in the real world). From skin and makeup collections that we can purchase at www.starley.com, to offers for whole looks from www.adam-n-eve.co.uk or garments on offer at www.nafii.com/Kasi/PixelDolls. The choice is continuing to grow (the examples described are just a fraction of what is available) as does the huge range of prices for the services (all in Linden Dollars, the official currency of Second Life). There are also videogames that simulate real spaces, such as The Sims 2, where you can find fashion shows for well-known brands or shops. This is a new experience which brings us closer to the personality of the brands and their products. Major developments are also being made in another area of virtual reality, namely interactive guides. Virtual guides have the enormous advantage of being able to deal with an infinite number of visitors, in any language available in the system and enable the customisation of content according to the requirements of the visit.

Screenshots of the tutorial created by Robin Wood that shows how to produce a T-shirt with direct prints for our avatar in Second Life, based on 2D-generated graphics.

There are currently a large number of programs enabling users to live, travel and interact in virtual spaces, although few of them have the collaboration of fashion designers. However, some examples such as www.lindenllivestyles.com offer young designers the possibility of promoting their designs by dressing the characters in this game.

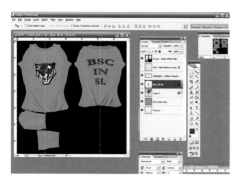

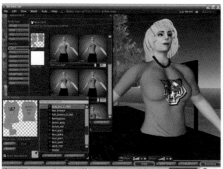

Image of ScarlettCast, an avatar created for the Second Life virtual platform.

It is not surprising that fashion companies have been attracted by this universe full of development opportunities, since one of the focuses of interest of this virtual world is the customisation of the avatars that represent us.

SECOND LIFE

Abbreviated as SL, Second Life is a virtual world that was launched in 2003, developed by Linden Research Inc. (known as Linden Lab), which has experienced a growing international interest since 2006. To use this program, you need to open an account and download a program called Second Life Viewer. When you register and log on, you become a 'resident' or AV, which is an abbreviation of avatar. The way in which residents interact through SL, which is one of the main attractions of this virtual world, is through the avatars (fully-configurable 3D characters), which enables users to become another person and enjoy, as the program name itself indicates, a second life. Its major attraction is the possibility of creating objects and interchanging a great variety of virtual products through an open market, whose local currency is the Linden Dollar ($L).

According to figures from March 2008, SL has approximately 13 million registered users (of which a high percentage is inactive). Programing in this virtual world is open and free. The SL code allows users to modify absolutely any aspect of the virtual world, from the character's eye colour and physical appearance to their movements and sounds. It also allows anything to be built in 3D, from a cube to a discotheque, a garden to a battlefield or a gun to a flower or a pair of Nike trainers. It is not surprising that fashion companies have been attracted to this universe full of development opportunities. In parallel, opportunities to create promotional spaces are endless. There are still few creations made by designers working exclusively in the virtual environment, but the first examples are beginning to emerge. The website www.lindenllifestyles.com encourages young designers to promote themselves in the virtual circuit, in order to benefit from the many advantages it offers.

THE SIMS 2 FASHION RUNWAY

The Fashion Runway connects the virtual world of The Sims 2 with the fashion world inspired by H&M, offering The Sims fans and all the *fashionistas* the unique opportunity to show off their creativity and personal style through their own designs, exhibiting their creations on the virtual catwalk hosted on the website www.TheSims2FashionRunway.com or www.hm.com/en. Everyone can participate in this fashion showcase, contributing their designs or voting for their favourites. Within the Sims 2 Fashion Runway, participants will have the opportunity for their creations to be valued by an H&M designer and, ultimately, for a garment inspired by their design to reach H&M stores in the future. The player can also go shopping. With The Sims 2 H&M Fashion Accessories you can choose from fashion basics inspired by H&M's real clothing collection, and create your own H&M shop. According to Jörgen Andersson, Director of Marketing for H&M: 'We are very excited that H&M is the first brand to enter The Sims world. For us, this pack is a fun opportunity to meet our customers in a new and exciting environment and to show our summer collection. The Sims' players are well-known for their creativity and skill; we are looking forward to seeing the participants' for our visual fashion catwalk.'

Steve Seabolt, H&M Vice President of Global Brand Development stated: 'Marrying a fashion company with the videogame recognised around the world will allow people to reflect their personalities and express their creativity. We couldn't imagine a more perfect match. Fashion inspires creativity in the same way videogames do. This brings new and exciting game content from two trusted brands that share the same global footprint and customer profile. From re-creations of dresses on the red carpet to fashions seen on the streets of Paris, we can't wait to see what The Sims community will come up with next!'

For more information on how to participate on this experience, visit:

www.TheSims2FashionRunway.com
www.hm.com/es

The Sims 2 Fashion Runway begins with the submission of designs by the participants. There are six themes on which to develop their summer creations. The first three are *Party Time*, *Skate Park* and *Street Wear*.

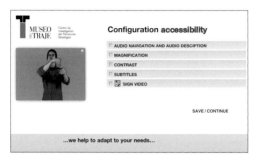

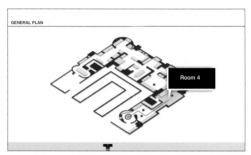

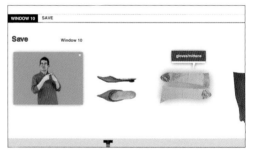

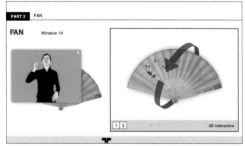

The images show various screenshots of the interface. Following the traditional approach, we find screenshots for setting up the accessibility resources, and others with maps of the museum and its rooms. The rest of the screenshots show the list of items in a display cabinet, re-creating items in 3D and in videos. All these display the floating window for sign language.

The GVAM is a R&D project of the Spanish Ministry of Industry, undertaken by the company Dos de Mayo, in collaboration with the Universidad Carlos III de Madrid, Fundación CNSE, Fundación ONCE and the General Directorate of Museums and Cultural Heritage of the Spanish Ministry of Culture.

GVAM – ACCESSIBLE VIRTUAL DIRECTORY FOR MUSEUM

The GVAM is revolutionising the way in which content is presented, respecting people with disabilities, as well as other visitors, so that museums are not just protagonists of the digital divide, but facilitate the incorporation of new technologies to the knowledge society. The first GVAM prototype has been initially developed for the *Museo del Traje* or Costume Museum of Madrid, which has collaborated intensively in the development and selection of content. The guide offers greater details of the context in which each item was produced, and specific information through different texts, photographs and videos. Some photographs allow us to examine the embroidery of costumes and accessories in detail, whereas in the videos we can see paintings or films in which they have been used, diagrams of their internal structure, geographical comparisons with costumes of other cultures or information about the production processes of the time. The GVAM screen size facilitates the composition of this content and its readability, especially for people with disabilities (with reduced vision) and for users who are deaf (who can comfortably read subtitles). The more powerful features offered by this media allow various multimedia resources to be shown simultaneously and include special features such as 3D games and re-creations.

Web 2.0

The term Web 2.0 was born halfway through 2004. It can be defined as the development of traditional tools towards Web applications focused on the end user. It differs from previous tools more as a change of attitude rather than a more sophisticated technology.

The original concept of the Web (in this context, called Web 1.0) was static HTML pages. In the 1990s, when the Internet began to grow, the Web was basically set up to inform with static pages, where the only thing that most users did or were able to do was click on different websites, without being actively involved in interaction or directing the information. The success of the .com depended on more dynamic websites (sometimes called Web 1.5) where the content management systems served dynamic HTML pages created in real time from an updated database. In both cases, obtaining hits (visits) and visual aesthetics were considered very important factors.

The concept of Web 2.0 became popular from its most representative applications: Wikipedia, YouTube, Flickr, WordPress, Blogger, MySpace, Facebook, OhMyNews and the surfeit of hundreds of tools trying to attract users and content-generators. The term Web 2.0 refers to a variety of applications and Internet pages, which use collective intelligence to provide interactive services on the network, giving the user control of their information. The Web 2.0 concept revolves around a series of satellite-terms that reinforce its development: social software, architecture of participation, user-generated content, etc. Hence, Web 2.0 is concerned with applications that generate collaboration and services which replace desktop applications. Many claim that what was the Internet has been reinvented, others speak of bubbles and investments, but the fact is that the natural evolution of the media has actually produced more interesting things for the end user.

The Anina Dress Up project was generated by the model Anina, founder of Anina.net and the company i2 technología (Brazil), both winners of the Nokia Champion prize.

To download the game for mobile phones:
http://mobi.aninadressup.com

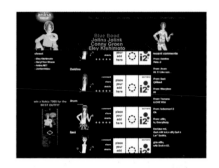

ANINA DRESS UP

This is the name of a highly interactive game, designed for mobile telephones, which includes information on the latest fashion industry news, advice and references to designers and international fashion labels. The aim of the game is to recreate the look proposed by the system in a short space of time, using your own clothing and items from the game library. The player's proposal is sent via GPRS to a virtual gallery where other participants can comment on and rate each proposal. This product reinforces user interactivity and participation, and allows both commercial brands and young designers to use the mobile telephone platform to show their creations to the general public.

360fashion.net is the first business network for the fashion industry. It was created in Paris in 2005 by the model Anina with associates such as as Nokia, Adobe, Eley Kishimoto, Fashion TV, Diane Pernet, and Viviane Blassel.

The company was founded to create a global network of contacts and businesses for designers, manufacturers and the media. Among its platforms you can find a variety of spaces: Web, mobile telephones, digital television, integrated under the concept of interactivity and participation.

360fashion.net services can be useful both for large, well-established companies and for emerging designers to build opportunities for international development.

Anina.net and 360fashion has offices in Shanghai, Paris, London, Amsterdam, and the US.

www.360fashion.net

BASIC PRINCIPLES

The constituent principles of Web 2.0 may be summarised in seven points: the worldwide web (www) as a work platform, the harnessing of collective intelligence, the management of databases as a core competence, the end of the cycle of software version updates, lightweight programming models together with the search for simplicity, software not limited by a single device, and enriching user experiences.

Over these pages we will take a look at some innovative experiences that are bringing fresh air to the international scene, experiences developed by established brands with large budgets and small-scale actions, but with an enormous capacity to impact on the current market.

Throughout the book, we have described interactive platforms that are of value for fashion design (blogs, wikis, etc.).The new Web 2.0 alternatives offer those working in fashion infinite possibilities for working and developing their projects through social networks, encouraging participation and interaction. These projects range from areas for exchanging information, opinions or experiences to spaces for uploading and sharing videos, tutorials or promoting individual activities. The professional brands (and designers) want to be close to their clients, and for this purpose create profiles in the large social networking platforms (MySpace, Facebook, Hi5) in order to gain proximity to the client and to try to establish channels of communication for promotional or research purposes.

The number of options is increasing along with the capacity to interact with other users. One of the latest initiatives that has had remarkable success is LinkedIn, a virtual network for professionals with a strong orientation towards job-hunting or exchanging experiences. LinkedIn lets you transfer your business contacts to the Internet and establish new professional relationships, with access to more than 25 million users in all the countries of the world.

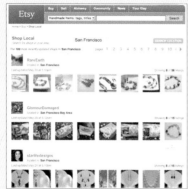

Images of the interface www.etsy.com

The Etsy platform includes comparisons of the communication, promotion and distribution of some of the products displayed.

The Etsy community has over 1,300,000 members and a total of 2.4 million products on display. It initially appeared as an exchange project and has become a business, with figures in 2008 reaching 56 million dollars in business transactions.

Etsy.com also offers information, seminars and tutorials, as well as information on all the events and actions organised in various parts of the international market.

ETSY.COM

Etsy.com is a virtual community that uses 2.0 technology and supports and enables an alternative market to the mass production of designs. It was created as a platform for designers to show their creations, share experiences and search for potential buyers. All the products displayed are hand-made and their production process respects environmental and ethical concerns. Etsy has generated new commercial discourses circulating alongside the traditional ones, which suit young designers who can't find a niche in the mass market.

www.etsy.com

Email, the most widespread online marketing tool

For some years, the biggest advertisers have been relying on news sent through the Internet. At present, email offers an unparalleled return in terms of customising of messages and accuracy of reports, etc. for any type of campaign: to win new clients, to strengthen client loyalty, and automatic relaunches.

The email method is very useful in campaigns aimed at informing the client of any aspect related to a project, and providing the opportunity to receive and consider potential buyers' responses in record time, without needing to commission market research or product-testing sessions. To optimise e-mailing and put it on a level with market research, which allows better predictions of customer responses to the launch of a product, it includes various advanced options:

- Personalisation of messages: fully customisable headers and footers, creation of blocks in the body of emails which allow communication to be adapted to different targets, etc.

- It has ultra-precise parameters: multilingual management of campaigns, specific link options to perfect its statistics, management of name deactivation, automatic or customised follow-up of content, creation of exclusion lists, etc.

- Provides appropriate analyses of the targets' behaviour: numerous dynamic tables and graphics that describe the full history of the campaigns, possible export of data, etc.

However, everything has its price, and faced with the massive abuse of email, users have reacted by restricting incoming mail. In general, all Internet users have anti-spam filters to combat the indiscriminate sending of advertising.

Interactive email campaigns for the client
Women'Secret, created by the design agency
Interactivo Minnim. The surprise effect and animation
are key factors for creating the necessary interaction
with the consumer.
www.minnim.tv

Direct marketing has not been unresponsive to this problem and
has developed 'permission marketing', which simply consists of
communicating only with users who have shown an interest, i.e.
users give consent to the intrusion. After all, this strategy, which
arises from the need to not tire the potential customer and to
seek efficient contact, at the same time allows information to be
obtained that is essential for accurate segmentation. In the same
way as email, mobile telephones, or more specifically SMS and
soon MMS, are becoming an indispensable communication tool
for young people. Nowadays all communications plans should
include a component of interactive viral marketing, mobile
websites and promotions or SMS games, or they will not be
effective. Both email and the SMS have the additional advantage
of being interactive and allowing segmentation of social
collectives according to groups of individuals. Research has
never been so simple and accurate, at least for products
targeted at teenagers and for companies whose marketing is
exclusively aimed at this group.

Advertising and promotional material

Digital processing of fashion images has taken over in a way that makes it truly inconceivable for us to see a model in an advertising campaign whose skin is full of marks, pores or facial hair. The possibilities of photographic retouching, filters and light settings, together with 3D design tools allows advertising images for both fashion products and for overall brand campaigns to be greatly improved.

Advertising images are no longer static and have become animated. The use of animated graphics created in 3D is increasingly common, although 2D graphics are still widely used for low bandwidths and real time applications that require quick rendering. The designs are developed with the help of design, modelling and rendering software. To create the illusion of motion, an image displayed on the screen is quickly replaced by a new image in a different still frame. This is an identical technique to that employed to create the illusion of movement in films and on television. For 2D vector animations, the rendering process is the key to the result. When the recordings are of real images, the still frames are converted to a different format or to a medium such as film or digital video. The frames can be rendered in real time as they are displayed to the end user. Animations that are transmitted via the Internet with low bandwidth (for example, 2D Flash, X3D) use programs on the user's computer to render the animation in real time as an alternative to transmission and for pre-loaded animations for high-speed links.

Images of the magazine *Untitled*, 2008.
© Michael Perry.

The *Untitled* project is a magazine that reflects the creative interests of Michael Perry and in which he can develop his personality as art director of the overall project.

www.midwestisbest.com

VIRTUAL OFFICES

Another important trend to note is that press offices i.e. the physical spaces, are being replaced by virtual offices on the Internet, where different professionals (fashion editors, stylists, editors, etc.) can log-on with a username and password to access specific information, texts, news or high-resolution images, request garments for photo sessions, movies or other promotional activities. These virtual press offices or pressrooms can be contacted from any geographical area at any time of day and from any terminal, greatly facilitating communication between the company or professional and the various media.

 PETPUNK STUDIO
The PetPunk studio is based in Vilnius, Lithuania. It is made up by Andrius Kirvela and Gediminas Siaulys, who work in art direction for graphic advertising and movies. They have carried out representative work for MTV, Vodafone, Cultures France, etc., and publications in magazines such as *Print. Net Digit, Etapes, Stash*. They are also authors of the books *Young European Graphic Designers* (DAAB) and *100@360. Graphic design's new global generation* (Laurence King).

www.petpunk.com

Apocalypse 2008 for the client Effigy.
AGENCY: Adell Taivas Ogilvy
ART DIRECTION: PetPunk

The concept of the Spring / Summer 08 campaign of the images created by the company PetPunk for the promotional campaign of the Effigy brand is *Apocalypse*. The models move within an atmosphere of graphic re-creation where the clothes are intermingled with volcanoes and giant waves (tsunamis), but with more humour than a spirit of catastrophe.

Digital video

Three inside portraits
CLIENTE Women'Secret
AGENCY Cla-se
PRODUCER Miss Wasabi
DIRECTOR Isabel Coixet

Audiovisual of Women'Secret brand image. Four real women talking about themselves. Four women with names and surnames, hopes, weaknesses, passions and doubts. Magali, Amandine, Natalia and Paola tell Women'Secret things they are not asked every day (and wouldn't tell just anyone).

Digital video is a very important media for the fashion industry. Not only do films convey the personality of a brand in a credible and efficient way, but they are extremely attractive for a market saturated with advertising information.

On occasions, a static image or advertising text does not manage to convey all the information, the range of feelings that a brand aims to transmit to the potential buyer. In these cases the use of video offers the director the opportunity of a few minutes to conceptualise their ideas and communicate them more effectively. For the consumer market, digital video systems first appeared in the QuickTime format (Apple Computer's architecture for time-based and streaming data formats), in about 1990. The initial tools for creating content were basic, requiring an analogue video source to be digitised to a computer-readable format. Although low-quality at first, digital video improved rapidly, firstly with the introduction of playback standards such as MPEG-1 and MPEG-2 (adopted for use in television transmission and DVD media), and then the introduction of the DV tape format allowing digital data to be recorded directly and simplifying the editing process, allowing non-linear editing systems to be used on desktop computers.

DIGITAL PUBLISHING

Digital video can be processed and edited on a non-linear editing station (a device built solely for editing video and audio). These often can import from both analogue and digital sources. They have no other features and are not intended to do anything other than edit videos. Digital video can also be edited on a personal computer which has the right hardware and software. Using a non-linear editing station, digital video can be manipulated to follow an order or sequence of video clips. Avid's software and hardware (www.avid.com) is almost synonymous with the professional non-linear editing station market, but Apple's Final Cut Pro (www.apple.com/es/finalcutstudio), Adobe Premiere (www.adobe.com/es/products/premiere) and other similar programs are popular and far more accessible to the market.

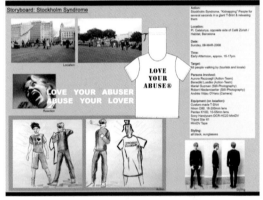

Stockholm Syndrome: *Acción Guerrilla en Barcelona.*
March 2008 (3:12 min).

AUTHORS Aurore Rezzoagli y Benedikt Luedke
PHOTOGRAPHY Andrès Vidau O'Hara, Mariel Guzman
and Robert Niederstaetter

'Guerrilla action' in which a T-shirt 'hero' kidnaps people
causing physical interaction with the victims. The video is
recorded in MiniDV format with post-production with the
application Apple iMovie. Subsequently, the video is
posted on the Youtube website
(www.youtube.com/watch?v=-YTW7KZxiFo) to start
the viral marketing action.

Nowadays, digital video is also used in modern mobile phones
and videoconferencing systems, for distributing videos on the
Internet, including through streaming, which is a term that refers
to seeing or hearing a file directly on a web page without having
to previously download it to your computer. It could be
described as 'click and view'. There are various video
compression systems – the main difference lies in the format
used for storage. DV video format uses its own codec while
editing. The MPEG2 compression system is used almost
exclusively for DVDs, whereas to view videos on the Internet
other formats are used, such as Windows Media, MPEG2,
MPEG4, Real Media, and the more recent H.264 Sorenson video
codec. The most widely-used are MPEG4 and Windows Media.

TRANSPARENCY IN FASHION COMMUNICATION: THE EMERGENCE OF 'THE MAKING OF'

At this time, advertising has lost credibility as the means of communication change. People have learned to be sceptical about the objectivity of the media, which find themselves continually under pressure to compromise their impartiality. Despite a lack of trust in traditional advertising, consumers enjoy brands. They like a good advertisement on TV and enjoy searching for information about a new and interesting product or service. In this sense, 'making of' or 'behind the scenes' videos are the perfect tool to strengthen brand reputation and isolate its image from damaging attacks from the press or part of public opinion. If we look closely at the new promotional campaigns, they not only show us the result, but the entire process of gestation of the photo session, the collection or filming of the spot. The new consumer wants to know all the details, and brands are willing to reveal them. On many occasions these 'behind the scenes' videos shed light on issues that are important to the company. In this way, teams that use organic materials can provide all the information relating to the origin of their materials, companies that opt for fair trade and respect employment rights, i.e. they can back up their messages with pictures of the teams, the work process and conditions.

Fashion and innovation. A shared future

We began this book by highlighting in the introduction that those working in fashion are presented with an important challenge, of entering the world of innovative technologies and using them for support. Our objective at the end of the book is to make a strong petition for backing the development of research towards future advances in this field.

Digital media enable the maximum information to be gained through advanced search processes. Forums for exchanging information, tutorials, blogs and wikis can become the best allies for design students' on-going learning process. Knowledge is recycled and new, previously unimagined possibilities emerge.

Nowadays innovation confers sure and reliable added-value for career development, which will be increasingly marked by designers' capacity to adapt to the various creative and work environments. In a world in which the geopolitical and social situation changes every day, knowledge is at the forefront of the most dynamic sector of contemporary culture. We will not be able to signal a 'generation' of new designers if the tools do not match up to the momentum of their era.

Innovation implies the concept of new. Today's society requires needs new means of expression and media that reflect its especially distinctive characteristics. Like any new element, these will undergo the test of time; some projects will be successful and others only transient or minor.

Today's designers will establish the future courses of action, processes and developments. Monitoring information and its evolution will undoubtedly be sources of knowledge and examples for future societies.

The time may have arrived for the new generation of designers to impose their ways of representation; they need to have a voice in order to lead the change in the fashion industry. Fashion has always been an agile vehicle in reflecting the social reality of each era, and the fashion industry is undergoing a major restructuring which does yet not show signs of stabilising. Whilst the end of the process is unknown, through this book readers can take an active position in managing this change and incorporate their own methods and tools to the society and era in which they live.

ALEXANDRA ZAHAROVA
www.flickr.com/photos/25436168@n08

ANINA FASHION
www.360fashion.net

AURORE REZZOAGLI / BENEDIKT LUEDKE
www.youtube.com/watch?v=-ytw7kzxifo

BINGOSHOP
notariat 8, 08001 barcelona
tel. 34 93 317 68 83

BOBBY BREIDHOLT
www.breidholt.com
www.flickr.com/breidholt

CATALUNYA DISSENY INFORMÀTIC
www.catdis.com
www.textilstudio.com

CHRIS GRAY
www.weshallsee.co.uk

DANNY ROBERTS
www.iqons.com/danny+roberts

DEMANO
www.demano.net

DOMINGO AYALA
www.domingoayala.com

EL DELGADO BUIL
www.eldelgadobuil.com

F-CUT BY FREITAG
www.freitag.ch/f-cut

FUTURE CONCEPT LAB
www.futureconceptlab.com

GERBER TECHNOLOGY
www.gerbertechnology.com

GISELA INTIMATES
carril de guetara 38, 29004 málaga
www.gisela.com

GUÍA VIRTUAL ACCESIBLE PARA MUSEOS
www.gvam.es

HEIDI.COM
www.heidi.com

ÍCARO NÉSTOR IBAÑEZ ARRICIVITA
www.myspace.com/icaroh

JACKLYN LARYEA
www.jackielaryea.com

JOAN CODINA
www.codinaorfebres.com

KERSTIN WACKER
www.wacker1.com

LEOLUCA ESCOBAR (AKA TERESA HU)
www.leolucaescobar.com

LECTRA
vía de los poblados 1 −1º planta
28033 madrid
www.lectra.com

LEONA CLARKE
www.leonaclarke.co.uk

MARCOS ZERENE (AKA FORMATBRAIN)
www.flickr.com/people/formatbrain

MARIA BALASHOWA (AKA M.BEE)
www.flickr.com/photos/balashowa/

MARILUZ VIDAL
www.mariluzvidal.com

MICHAEL PERRY
www.midwestisbest.com

MIGUEL CABALLERO
mi-caballero@hotmail.com
minnim, interactive agency
www.minnim.tv

MY VIRTUAL MODEL INC
www.mvm.com

NADJA GIROD
www.smil.biz

OPTITEX
www.optitex.com

PETER WILSON (AKA GOONISM)
goonism@yahoo.co.uk

PETPUNK
www.petpunk.com

PRIVALIA.COM
www.privalia.com

RAÜL VÁZQUEZ
www.myspace.com/raul_vazquez

RICARD DOMINGO,
creative direction in jewellery
www.ricardomingo.com

RHINOGOLD
www.rhinogold.com
www.tdmsolutions.com

SHIRLEYMOON
www.shirleymoon.com
www.thechipfactory.co.uk

TEACHHEART
www.teach-heart.com
www.thgallery.fr

THREADLESS
www.threadless.com

VERENA GROTO
www.appealtotheeye.blogspot.com

WGSN LTD. (SPAIN AND PORTUGAL)
Aribau 175, 3-2B
08036 Barcelona
Tel 34 93 414 47 56
www.wgsn.com

WOMEN'SECRET
www.womensecret.com

The development of this book would not have been possible without the active and disinterested contribution from individuals and companies from all the capitals of the world, who have supported us by providing their work, comments and real experiences. All the team that has participated in this book acknowledges the helpfulness of all those who have contributed and the quality of their work.

Below are a selection of links to a group of the
most prominent websites in which the reader will be able to
obtain information, share pictures or simply download
mini-applications that will facilitate their work.

WEBSITES, WEBLOGS AND PHOTOBLOGS FASHION FAVORITES

http://www.ashadedviewonfashion.com
http://www.frills.com
http://www.hel-looks.com
http://www.ponystep.com
http://www.cutoutandkeep.net
http://www.narzib-memorimento.blogspot.com
http://perezhilton.com
http://www.nylonmag.com/?section=blog
http://jcreport.com/blog
http://blog.guerrillacomm.com
http://www.icanteachyouhowtodoit.com
http://hypebeast.com
http://thesartorialist.blogspot.com
http://www.adbusters.org
http://stylebubble.typepad.com
http://highsnobiety.blogspot.com
http://devilwearszara.elleblogs.es
http://www.threadless.com/blogs
http://www.360fashion.net
http://www.myfashionlife.com
http://www.dailycandy.com
http://www.etsy.com
http://fashiontribes.typepad.com
http://formatmag.com
http://www.faceyourpockets.com
http://appealtotheeye.blogspot.coa

http://www.prettypretty.be
http://www.thecoolhunter.net
http://formatmag.com
http://www.wgsn.com

WEBSITES WITH FREE USE OF PHOTOGRAPHS

http://gallery.hd.org
http://shutterstock.com
http://ace-clipart.com
http://openphoto.net
http://morguefile.com
http://www.sxc.hu
http://www.freedigitalphotos.net
http://www.woophy.com
http://www.pixelperfectdigital.com/free_stock_photos
http://www.dreamstime.com/free-photos
http://www.everystockphoto.com
http://www.stockvault.net
http://www.freepixels.com
http://www.freerangestock.com
http://www.imageafter.com
http://www.aboutpixel.de
http://www.freephotosweb.com/freephotosweb
http://www.twicepix.net/imgdb/index.php
http://www.bigfoto.com

http://www.pixelio.de
http://www.freeimages.co.uk
http://www.bancodeimagem.com.br
http://www.freephotobank.org/main.php
http://www.public-domain-photos.com
http://www.abstractinfluence.com
http://www.freefoto.com
http://www.unices.org
http://amygdela.com/stock
http://www.zurb.net/zurbphotos
http://energy.star29.net/store
http://www.stickstock.com
http://www.dieblen.de
http://www.graphicsarena.com
http://www.tripalbum.net
http://www.oneodddude.net
http://majesticimagery.com
http://www.designpacks.com
http://www.farmphoto.com
http://www.bajstock.com/main.htm
http://www.essendemme.com/stock_photos
http://www.creativity103.com
http://www.piotrpix.com
http://www.trulyfreestock.com
http://www.lightmatter.net/gallery
http://freestockphotos.com
http://www.ilovestockphotography.net
http://www.imagetemple.com

WEBSITES WITH FREE FONTS FOR FREE USE

http://www.floodfonts.com
http://www.eutypoce.com
http://www.stencilrevolution.com
http://www.smeltery.net
http://www.josbuivenga.demon.nl
http://www.neo2.es/blog/category/typography

OTHER WEBSITES OF INTEREST

http://rapidshare.com
http://www.yousendit.com
http://moodstream.gettyimages.com
https://delicious.com
http://facebook.com
http://secondlife.com
http://myspace.com
http://www.tuenti.com
http://fontstruct.fontshop.com
http://www.reyes-infografica.com